Phonemic Awareness in Young Children

Phonemic Awareness in Young Children

A Classroom Curriculum

Marilyn Jager Adams, Ph.D.
Harvard University
Cambridge, Massachusetts

Barbara R. Foorman, Ph.D.
University of Texas
Houston, Texas

Ingvar Lundberg, Ph.D.
Göteborg University
Göteborg, Sweden

and

Terri Beeler, Ed.D.
University of Houston
Houston, Texas

·P A U L ·H ·
BROOKES
PUBLISHING C⁰ ®

Baltimore • London • Sydney

Paul H. Brookes Publishing Co.
Post Office Box 10624
Baltimore, Maryland 21285-0624
www.brookespublishing.com

Typeset by A.W. Bennett, Hartland, Vermont.
Manufactured in the United States of America by
V.G. Reed & Sons, Inc., Louisville, Kentucky.

Illustrations by Kathleen Gray Farthing.

First printing, September 1997.
Second printing, January 1998.
Third printing, April 1998.
Fourth printing, June 1998.
Fifth printing, December 1998.
Sixth printing, June 1999.
Seventh printing, October 1999.
Eighth printing, June 2000.
Ninth printing, June 2001.
Tenth printing, December 2001.
Eleventh printing, August 2002.

Twelfth printing, April 2003.
Thirteenth printing, October 2003.
Fourteenth printing, August 2004.

Library of Congress Cataloging-in-Publication Data

Phonemic awareness in young children : a classroom curriculum /
    Marilyn Jager Adams . . . [et al.].
       p.   cm.
      Includes bibliographical references and index.
      ISBN 1-55766-321-1
      1. Children—United States—Language.   2. English language—Phonemics—Study and teaching
(Early childhood)—United States.   3. Early childhood education—Activity programs—United States.
4. Curriculum planning—United States.   I. Adams, Marilyn Jager.
    LB1139.L3P46   1998
    372.46'5—dc21
                                         97-21682
                                             CIP

British Library Cataloguing in Publication data are available from the British Library.

Contents

About the Authors

Marilyn Jager Adams, Ph.D., a visiting scholar at the Harvard University Graduate School of Education, received her Ph.D. in cognitive and developmental psychology from Brown University in 1975 and has been working on issues of education and cognition ever since. In 1995, she was presented with the American Educational Research Association's (AERA) Sylvia Scribner Award for Outstanding Contribution to Education through Research.

In addition to a number of chapter and journal articles, Dr. Adams is the author of the landmark synthesis of research on reading and its acquisition, *Beginning to Read: Thinking and Learning About Print* (MIT Press, 1990). She is also the principal author of several classroom resources, including the kindergarten and primary levels of *Collections for Young Scholars* (SRA/McGraw-Hill, 1995) and *Odyssey: A Curriculum for Thinking* (Charlesbridge, 1986), an experimentally validated program on thinking skills that was originally developed for Venezuelan barrio students.

Dr. Adams was Vice President (1995–1997) of AERA and a member of the Study Committee for the National Academy of Sciences' Committee on the Prevention of Reading Difficulties in Young Children, the College Boards' Advisory Committee for Research and Development, and the planning committee for the 1992 National Assessment of Educational Progress in Reading. She is a member of the national advisory boards for the Consortium on Reading Excellence (CORE), the Orton/International Dyslexia Society, the Society for the Scientific Study of Reading, and the Neuhaus Education Center. She is on the Literacy Advisory Board for *Sesame Street* and for *Between the Lions,* a forthcoming television show on reading for 4- to 7-year-olds, and has also worked on early literacy products with a number of educational software groups including Apt Productions, Breakthrough, Cast, Disney Interactive, Microsoft, Sunburst/Software for Success, 7th Level, and The Waterford Institute.

Barbara R. Foorman, Ph.D., earned her doctorate at the University of California–Berkeley. She is Professor of Pediatrics and Director of the Center for Academic and Reading Skills at the University of Texas–Houston Medical School and Principal Investigator of the grant funded by the National Institute of Child Health and Human Development (NICHD), "Early Interventions for Children with Reading Problems." In addition to many chapters and journal articles on topics related to language and reading development, she is the editor of *Reading Acquisition: Cultural Constraints and Cognitive Universals* (Lawrence Erlbaum Associates, 1986). She is on the editorial board of *Journal of Learning Disabilities* and has guest edited special issues of *Scientific Studies of Reading, Linguistics and Education* and *Journal of Learning Disabilities.* Dr. Foorman has been actively involved in outreach to the schools and to the general public, having chaired Houston Independent School District's Committee on a Balanced Approach to Reading and having testified before the California and Texas legislatures and the Texas State Board of Education Long-Range Planning Committee. Dr. Foorman is also a member of the National Academy of Sciences'

Committee on the Prevention of Reading Difficulties in Young Children, the board of the Society for the Scientific Study of Reading, the Consortium on Reading Excellence (CORE), and several local reading efforts.

Ingvar Lundberg, Ph.D., was first trained as a school teacher and served in inner-city schools in Stockholm, Sweden. Later, he entered an academic career and became Professor of Developmental Psychology at the University of Ume. He has published a dozen books, primarily in Scandinavian languages and a large number of scientific articles, particularly in the field of reading and language development. He served on the steering committee of the largest survey of reading achievement in the world, including more than 30 countries. He is a fellow of several academies and learned societies and serves on the editorial board of a number of scientific journals. He is currently affiliated with the Department of Psychology at Göteborg University, Göteborg, Sweden, where he directs a research program on communication disabilities.

Terri Beeler, Ed.D., has more than 20 years of experience in education, in both teaching and administration. Dr. Beeler is Assistant Professor in the Department of Urban Education at the University of Houston's downtown campus. Within the responsibilities of that position, she is one of the coordinators of a totally field-based teacher education program, which allows her to work with both preservice and in-service teachers and also continue to be in classrooms with children. In addition, she does a great deal of staff development and consultant work in the area of early literacy development, specifically phonemic awareness and guided reading. She is also a co-editor of the *State of Reading,* the journal of the Texas State Reading Association, and author of *I Can Read, I Can Write: Creating a Print-Rich Environment* (Creative Teaching Press, 1993).

Preface

Phonemic awareness is the buzz word of our times. Children who are aware of phonemes move easily and productively into inventive spelling and reading. Children who are not aware of phonemes are at serious risk of failing to learn to read. Educators who teach phonemic awareness have found that doing so accelerates the reading and writing growth of the entire classroom even as it reduces the incidence of children with reading delay. They have also found that attending to children's phonemic awareness removes phonics from the realm of drill and skill and makes it learnable and interesting to their students.

By now, everyone involved in the education of young children has heard these proclamations over and over. Most are convinced of the importance of monitoring and supporting their students' phonemic awareness. Even so, few have been given any real, concrete help in this venture. What exactly is phonemic awareness? And exactly how might one go about supporting it in the kindergarten or first-grade classroom?

In developing this book, our intention was to help fill this gap. Our introduction in Chapter 1 attempts to make comprehensible the nature of phonemic awareness, how it relates to reading and writing acquisition, and why it is tricky. Similarly, each set of activities is prefaced with an explanation of their rationale in terms both of linguistics and literacy development. Most of all, however, we expect that by trying these activities with your students and carefully watching their reactions and growth, you will more fully understand the nature of phonemic awareness.

This book is based on the Lundberg, Frost, and Petersen (1988) program developed in Sweden and Denmark. Beyond translating, we have added, subtracted, and modified activities in light of more recent research to better suit the tempo and culture of American classrooms. Because we wanted to make sure that these efforts served to adjust but not damage the product, we evaluated it in 23 kindergarten classrooms in Houston over a 3-year period, assessing and confirming the children's growth in phonemic awareness and incorporating feedback from the teachers about the curriculum. We are delighted to make this curriculum available to teachers throughout the English-speaking world.

REFERENCE

Lundberg, I., Frost, J., & Petersen, O.P. (1988). Effects of an extensive program for stimulating phonological awareness in preschool children. *Reading Research Quarterly, 23,* 264–284.

Acknowledgments

In the end, the activities collected here are the result of many people's collaboration. Research on this phonemic awareness curriculum was supported by Grants No. HD30995, "Early Interventions for Children with Reading Problems," and HD28172, "Detecting Reading Problems by Modeling Individual Growth," from the National Institute of Child Health and Human Development (NICHD). Investigators were Drs. Barbara Foorman, David Francis, and Jack Fletcher. We would like to acknowledge Debbie Winikates, Angeliki Mouzaki, Pat McEnery, Richard Williams, and Christopher Scatschneider for their help in these investigations.

We would also like to thank the kindergarten teachers at Liestman and Boone Elementary Schools in Alief Independent School District and the kindergarten teachers in Alcott, Douglass, Texas Southern University/Houston Independent School District (TSU/HISD) Lab School, and Turner Elementary Schools in the Houston Independent School District who field-tested this curriculum in their classrooms and provided us with invaluable feedback, especially Sunni Markowitz. We also thank the kindergarten children at those schools for helping us understand how young children think about language.

We would especially like to thank Ase Huggins for her invaluable help in translating the curriculum from Danish and Elaine Niefeld and Lisa Rapisarda for their patience and excellent editorial support.

With love to little readers and their teachers everywhere

Phonemic Awareness in Young Children

1 The Nature and Importance of Phonemic Awareness

Before children can make any sense of the alphabetic principle, they must understand that those sounds that are paired with the letters are one and the same as the sounds of speech. For those of us who already know how to read and write, this realization seems very basic, almost transparent. Nevertheless, research shows that the very notion that spoken language is made up of sequences of these little sounds does not come naturally or easily to human beings.

The small units of speech that correspond to letters of an alphabetic writing system are called *phonemes*. Thus, the awareness that language is composed of these small sounds is termed *phonemic awareness*. Research indicates that, without direct instructional support, phonemic awareness eludes roughly 25% of middle-class first graders and substantially more of those who come from less literacy-rich backgrounds. Furthermore, these children evidence serious difficulty in learning to read and write (see Adams, 1990, for a review).

Why is awareness of phonemes so difficult? The problem, in large measure, is that people do not attend to the sounds of phonemes as they produce or listen to speech. Instead, they process the phonemes automatically, directing their active attention to the meaning and force of the utterance as a whole. The challenge, therefore, is to find ways to get children to notice the phonemes, to discover their existence and separability. Fortunately, many of the activities involving rhyme, rhythm, listening, and sounds that have long been enjoyed with preschool-age children are ideally suited for this purpose. In fact, with this goal in mind, all such activities can be used more effectively toward helping children to develop phonemic awareness.

The purpose of this book is to provide concrete activities that stimulate the development of phonemic awareness in the preschool or elementary classroom. It is based on a program originally developed and validated by Lundberg, Frost, and Petersen (1988) in Sweden and Denmark. After translating and adapting it for U.S. classrooms, we field-tested it with kindergarten students and teachers in two schools receiving Title I funds. We, too, found that kindergartners developed the ability to analyze words into sounds significantly more quickly than kindergartners who did not have this program (Foorman, Francis, Beeler, Winikates, & Fletcher, 1997; Foorman, Francis, Shaywitz, Shaywitz, & Fletcher, 1997). This ability to analyze words into sounds is exactly the skill that promotes successful reading in first grade (Wagner, Torgesen, & Rashotte, 1994).

WHAT RESEARCH SAYS ABOUT PHONEMIC AWARENESS

Although a number of different types of linguistic awareness are, in one way or another, presupposed in the dialogues and activities of beginning reading instruction, preschool-age children's awareness of phonemes—of the speech sounds that correspond roughly to individual letters—has been shown to hold singular predictive power, statistically accounting for as much as 50% of the variance in their reading proficiency at the end of first grade (Blachman, 1991; Juel, 1991; Stanovich, 1986; Wagner et al., 1994). Furthermore, faced with an alphabetic script, a child's level of phonemic awareness on entering school is widely held to be the strongest single determinant of the success that she or he will experience in learning to read—or, conversely, the likelihood that she or he will fail (Adams, 1990; Stanovich, 1986).

Measures of preschool-age children's level of phonemic awareness strongly predict their future success in learning to read; this has been demonstrated not only among English students but also among Swedish (Lundberg, Olofsson, & Wall, 1980); Norwegian (Høien, Lundberg, Stanovich, & Bjaalid, 1995); Spanish (deManrique & Gramigna, 1984); French (Alegria, Pignot, & Morais, 1982); Italian (Cossu, Shankweiler, Liberman, Tola, & Katz, 1988); Portuguese (Cardoso-Martins, 1995); and Russian students (Elkonin, 1973). Measures of schoolchildren's ability to attend to and manipulate phonemes strongly correlate with their reading success through the twelfth grade (Calfee, Lindamood, & Lindamood, 1973). Poorly developed phonemic awareness distinguishes economically disadvantaged preschoolers from their more advantaged peers (Wallach, Wallach, Dozier, & Kaplan, 1977) and has been shown to be characteristic of adults with literacy problems in the United States (Liberman, Rubin, Duques, & Carlisle, 1985); Portugal (Morais, Cary, Alegria, & Bertelson, 1979); England (Marcel, 1980); and Australia (Byrne & Ledez, 1983). Indeed, among readers of alphabetic languages, those who are successful invariably have phonemic awareness, whereas those who lack phonemic awareness are invariably struggling (Foorman, Francis, Beeler, et al., 1997; Foorman, Francis, Fletcher, Winikates, & Mehta, 1997; Foorman, Francis, Shaywitz, et al., 1997; Stanovich, 1986; Tunmer & Nesdale, 1985).

Knowing that so many children lack phonemic awareness and that phonemic awareness is critical to learning to read and write an alphabetic script, we begin to see the importance of making a place for its instruction. In fact, research clearly shows that phonemic awareness can be developed through instruction and, furthermore, that doing so significantly accelerates children's subsequent reading and writing achievement

(Ball & Blachman, 1991; Blachman, Ball, Black, & Tangel, 1994; Bradley & Bryant, 1983; Byrne & Fielding-Barnsley, 1991, 1993, 1995; Castle, Riach, & Nicholson, 1994; Cunningham, 1990; Lundberg et al., 1988; Wallach & Wallach, 1979; Williams, 1980).

ABOUT THE STRUCTURE OF LANGUAGE

In order to build phonemic awareness in *all* children, classroom teachers should know a little about the structure of language, especially phonology. *Phonology* is the study of the unconscious rules governing speech-sound production. In contrast, *phonetics* is the study of the way in which speech sounds are articulated, and *phonics* is the system by which symbols represent sounds in an alphabetic writing system. (For summaries of phonetic symbols and classifications of consonants and vowels in English, see Tables 1–3 and Figure 1 in Appendix A.)

Phonological rules constrain speech-sound production for biological and environmental reasons. Biological constraints are due to the limitations of human articulatory-motor production. For example, humans are not able to produce the high-frequency vocalizations of whales. Other constraints on our ability to produce speech have to do with the way our brains classify and perceive the minimal units of sound that make a difference to meaning—the units we call *phonemes*.

The differences between the sounds of two phonemes are often very subtle: Compare /b/ with /p/. Yet, these subtle differences in sound can signal dramatic differences in meaning: Compare *bat* with *pat*. Fortunately, because phonemes are the basic building blocks of spoken language, babies become attuned to the phonemes of their native language in the first few months of life. However, this sensitivity to the sounds of the phonemes and the differences between them is not conscious. It is deeply embedded in the subattentional machinery of the language system.

Phonemes are also the units of speech that are represented by the letters of an alphabetic language. Thus, developing readers must learn to separate these sounds, one from another, and to categorize them in a way that permits understanding of how words are spelled. It is this sort of explicit, reflective knowledge that falls under the rubric of *phonemic awareness*. Conscious awareness of phonemes is distinct from the built-in sensitivity that supports speech production and reception. Unfortunately, phonemic awareness is not easy to establish.

Part of the difficulty in acquiring phonemic awareness is that, from word to word and speaker to speaker, the sound of any given phoneme can vary considerably. These sorts of variations in spoken form that do *not* indicate a difference in meaning are referred to as *allophones* of a phoneme. For example, in the northern part of the United States, the pronunciation of *grease* typically rhymes with *peace*, whereas in parts of the South, it rhymes with *sneeze*. Similarly, the pronunciations of the vowels vary greatly across regions, dialects, and individuals. Alternately, variations in spoken form sometimes eliminate phonetic distinctions between phonemes. Thus, for some people, the words *pin* and *pen* are pronounced differently with distinct medial sounds corresponding to their distinct vowels. For other people, however, these words are phonetically indistinguishable, leaving context as the only clue to meaning. Indeed, because of variations in the language, even linguists find it difficult to say exactly how many phonemes there are in English; answers vary from 44 to 52.

It is also important to note that phonemes are not spoken as separate units. Rather, they are *co-articulated;* that is, when we speak, we fuse the phonemes together into a syllabic unit. For example, when we say *bark* aloud, we do not produce four distinct phonemes: /b/, /a/, /r/, /k/. Instead, our pronunciation of the initial consonant is influenced by the medial vowel, and the medial vowel is influenced by the consonants before and after it. Thus, we talk about *r-controlled vowels* like the "ar" in *bark.* Similarly, we speak of *nasalized vowels* before nasal consonants, such as in the words *and, went,* and *gym.* Because these vowels are assimilated into the following consonant in speech, most children have special difficulty representing them as distinct phonemes in reading and spelling, such that, for example, *went* might be read or spelled as W-E-T.

Consonants as well as vowels are affected by co-articulation. Consider /t/ and /d/. Say the words *write* and *ride.* The /t/ and /d/ sound distinct in these two words. However, now say *writer* and *rider.* Now the medial /t/ and /d/ phonemes are reduced to a common phoneme (called a tongue flap). Not surprisingly, children are likely to spell *writer* as R-I-D-R. Furthermore, /t/ and /d/ are affected by /r/ in consonant blends. Pronounce the following pairs of words: *tuck-truck; task-trash; dunk-drunk; dagger-dragon.* Children notice the change in /t/ and /d/ when followed by /r/ and represent the phonetic detail with spellings of C-H-R-A-N for *train* and J-R-A-G-N for *dragon.* (In linguistic terms, the alveolar consonants /t/ and /d/ are palatalized and are articulated much like the affricates in the initial sounds of *chock* and *jock.* See Table 2 in Appendix A.)

The phonological awareness activities in this curriculum ask children to listen to the sameness, difference, number, and order of speech sounds. As the previous examples illustrate, such activities can become difficult when the phonetic level of speech does not relate cleanly or directly to the phonemic level. Yet, it is ultimately the phonemic level we are after because it is awareness of phonemes that allows children to understand how the alphabet works—an understanding that is essential to learning to read and spell.

For more information on phonology, we recommend Fromkin and Rodman (1993) and Parker and Riley (1994). For more information on how phonology relates to the teaching and learning of reading and spelling, we recommend Hull (1985), Moats (1995), and Treiman (1993). For more information on how to work with children who have extreme difficulty with speech-sound production, we recommend Lindamood and Lindamood (1975). For further information or assistance in working with these children, we add that speech-language pathologists can be very helpful. Their training provides them with in-depth understanding of phonology as well as expressive and receptive syntax (i.e., the rule system by which words may be ordered in phrases and sentences).

PHONEMIC AWARENESS IN YOUNG CHILDREN: A CLASSROOM CURRICULUM

The remainder of this curriculum presents a program of games and activities that are intended for use with kindergarten, first-grade, and special education students (see Appendices B and C). A list of commercially available resources to use in presenting these games is provided in Appendix D.

Notes to the Special Education Teacher

Research reveals that poorly developed phonemic awareness is the core difficulty for a large proportion of children who are having difficulty learning to read. Thus, these language games may also be useful in the special education program. Just as with the original program, it is important to work with the games regularly and to revisit each frequently until it is mastered and can be extended. In special education classrooms, however, the program should be initiated at the child's identified level of difficulty and continued from there. Also, unlike the original program, one particular area should be all but mastered before introducing activities from the next area. Syllables, for example, should be firmly established before moving on to initial sounds.

The Structure of the Program

The underlying structure of the program follows the accepted teaching methodology of introducing, practicing, extending, and revisiting the various phonemic tasks. New phonemic challenges are presented in a gradual, step-by-step progression, with new challenges building on those previously introduced and practiced. Developed to be "user friendly" for teachers, the program includes objectives, explanations for implementation, and cautions as to possible problems as well as a suggested schedule for visiting and revisiting the various activities.

The activities themselves have been designed in such a way that teachers can assess their students' progress by informally observing their responses and involvement. In particular, teachers are urged to switch frequently but unpredictably between soliciting responses from the whole group and from individuals of their designation. This is a dual-purpose strategy. While affording the teacher a day-to-day means of assessing individual progress, it also serves to motivate the children to participate actively and thoughtfully.

In addition, the program has been designed with careful attention to the developmental needs of young children. All sessions are brief, containing no more than two or three activities. All of the games involve some level of active participation, giving the children opportunities to make up nonsense words or rhymes and actions of their own creation. In addition, many of the games are designed around physical activities. Furthermore, some of the games are delightfully silly, and all are designed to be engaging for the children. Although this dimension proved to be most difficult to translate (among other obstacles, many of the Danish materials are mildly inappropriate by American standards), we must still stress its importance. Not only does this program entertain children, it also captures their interest and provides them with materials that they will want to remember, think about, and repeat, so that the learning will extend beyond the immediate teaching context in thought and time.

Finally, a note is in order about the adaptations and adjustments that we made in putting together this version of the program. First, and most obvious, literal translation of language play is not possible. Necessarily, we have replaced the original poems and songs and reinvented the word lists to recapture in English the spirit of the intended phonological play. In addition, we have modified the activities in deference to structural differences between the languages or more recent research on the particular difficulties and priorities of American phonology. Second, in the interest of classroom management and teacher support, we have refined the instructions, added support material, and occasionally modified the play and dynamics of the games as guided by our field work. Third, and most important, we have added a whole new chapter to the program (Chapter 9: Introducing Letters and Spellings). The original program involved oral language play only. As such, the reading/writing advantage evidenced by Lundberg et al.'s (1988) young students offered strong validation of the advantages of training phonological awareness per se. Yet, the reason for training phonological awareness at all is to make spelling-sound correspondences more learnable when they are taught. In keeping with this philosophy, several more recent studies have demonstrated that the impact of phonemic awareness training on early reading and writing is enhanced still further when spelling-sound correspondences are developed alongside speech-sound correspondences (Ball & Blachman, 1990; Blachman et al., 1994; Byrne & Fielding-Barnsley, 1991, 1993, 1995; Hatcher, Hulme, & Ellis, 1994). It is important to note that doing so does not amount to a reversion to conventional phonics, for the letter-sound correspondences are not presented for rote memorization in and of themselves. Instead, they are built into the phonemic awareness activities in a way that ensures that the children's growing appreciation of the phonemic structure of the language will yield a confident, productive understanding of the logic of its written representation.

REFERENCES

Adams, M.J. (1990). *Beginning to read: Thinking and learning about print.* Cambridge, MA: MIT Press.

Alegria, J., Pignot, E., & Morais, J. (1982). Phonetic analysis of speech and memory codes in beginning readers. *Memory and Cognition, 10,* 451–456.

Ball, E.W., & Blachman, B.A. (1991). Does phoneme segmentation training in kindergarten make a difference in early word recognition and developmental spelling? *Reading Research Quarterly, 26,* 49–66.

Blachman, B.A. (1991). Getting ready to read: Learning how print maps to speech. In J.F. Kavanagh (Ed.), *The language continuum: From infancy to literacy* (pp. 41–62). Timonium, MD: York Press.

Blachman, B.A., Ball, E.W., Black, R.S., & Tangel, D.M. (1994). Kindergarten teachers develop phoneme awareness in low-income, inner-city classrooms: Does it make a difference? *Reading and Writing, 6,* 1–18.

Bradley, L., & Bryant, P.E. (1983). Categorizing sounds and learning to read: A causal connection. *Nature, 301,* 419–421.

Byrne, B., & Fielding-Barnsley, R. (1991). Evaluation of a program to teach phonemic awareness to young children. *Journal of Educational Psychology, 83,* 451–455.

Byrne, B., & Fielding-Barnsley, R. (1993). Evaluation of a program to teach phonemic awareness to young children: A 1-year follow-up. *Journal of Educational Psychology, 85,* 104–111.

Byrne, B., & Fielding-Barnsley, R. (1995). Evaluation of a program to teach phonemic awareness to young children: A 2- and 3-year follow-up and a new preschool trial. *Journal of Educational Psychology, 87,* 488–503.

Byrne, B., & Ledez, J. (1983). Phonological awareness in reading disabled adults. *Australian Journal of Psychology, 35,* 185–197.

Calfee, R.C., Lindamood, P.E., & Lindamood, C.H. (1973). Acoustic-phonetic skills and reading: Kindergarten through 12th grade. *Journal of Educational Psychology, 64,* 293–298.

Cardoso-Martins, C. (1995). Sensitivity to rhymes, syllables, and phonemes in literacy acquisition in Portuguese. *Reading Research Quarterly, 30,* 808–828.

Castle, J.M., Riach, J., & Nicholson, T. (1994). Getting off to a better start in reading and spelling: The effects of phonemic awareness instruction within a whole-language program. *Journal of Educational Psychology, 86,* 350–359.

Cossu, G., Shankweiler, D., Liberman, I.Y., Tola, G., & Katz, L. (1988). Awareness of phonological segments and reading ability in Italian children. *Applied Psycholinguistics, 9,* 1–16.

Cunningham, A.E. (1990). Explicit versus implicit instruction in phonemic awareness. *Journal of Experimental Child Psychology, 50,* 429–444.

deManrique, A.M.B., & Gramigna, S. (1984). La segmentacion fonologica y silabica en niños de preescolar y primer grado [The phonological segmentation of syllables in nine first-year preschoolers]. *Lectura y Vida, 5,* 4–13.

Elkonin, D.B. (1973). U.S.S.R. In J. Downing (Ed.), *Comparative reading* (pp. 551–579). New York: Macmillan.

Foorman, B.R., Francis, D.J., Beeler, T., Winikates, D., & Fletcher, J.M. (1997). Early interventions for children with reading problems: Study designs and preliminary findings. *Learning Disabilities: A Multidisciplinary Journal, 8,* 63–71.

Foorman, B.R., Francis, D.J., Fletcher, J.M., Winikates, D., & Mehta, P. (1997). Early interventions for children with reading problems. *Scientific Studies of Reading, 1*(3), 255–276.

Foorman, B.R., Francis, D.J., Shaywitz, S.E., Shaywitz, B.A., & Fletcher, J.M. (1997). The case for early reading interventions. In B. Blachman (Ed.), *Foundations of reading acquisition and dyslexia: Implications for early intervention* (pp. 243–264). Mahwah, NJ: Lawrence Erlbaum Associates.

Fromkin, V., & Rodman, R. (1993). *An introduction to language* (4th ed.). New York: Holt, Rinehart & Winston.

Hatcher, P.J., Hulme, C., & Ellis, A.W. (1994). Ameliorating early reading failure by integrating the teaching of reading and phonological skills: The phonological linkage hypothesis. *Child Development, 65,* 41–57.

Høien, T., Lundberg, I., Stanovich, K.E., & Bjaalid, I. (1995). Components of phonological awareness. *Reading and Writing, 7,* 171–188.

Hull, M. (1985). *Phonics for the teacher of reading* (4th ed.). Columbus, OH: Charles E. Merrill.

Juel, C. (1991). Beginning reading. In R. Barr, M.L. Kamil, P.B. Mosenthal, & P.D. Pearson (Eds.), *Handbook of reading research* (Vol. 2, pp. 759–788). New York: Longman.

Liberman, I.Y., Rubin, H., Duques, S., & Carlisle, J. (1985). Linguistic abilities and spelling proficiency in kindergartners and adult poor spellers. In D.B. Gray & J.F. Kavanagh (Eds.), *Biobehavioral measures of dyslexia* (pp. 163–176). Timonium, MD: York Press.

Lindamood, C., & Lindamood, P. (1975). *The A.D.D. Program: Auditory Discrimination in Depth.* Austin, TX: PRO-ED.

Lundberg, I., Frost, J., & Petersen, O.P. (1988). Effects of an extensive program for stimulating phonological awareness in preschool children. *Reading Research Quarterly, 23,* 264–284.

Lundberg, I., Olofsson, Å., & Wall, S. (1980). Reading and spelling skills in the first school years predicted from phonemic awareness skills in kindergarten. *Scandinavian Journal of Psychology, 21,* 159–173.

Marcel, A. (1980). Phonological awareness and phonological representation: Investigation of a specific spelling problem. In U. Frith (Ed.), *Cognitive processes in spelling* (pp. 373–403). New York: Academic Press.

Moats, L.C. (1995). *Spelling: Development, disability, and instruction.* Timonium, MD: York Press.

Morais, J., Cary, L., Alegria, J., & Bertelson, P. (1979). Does awareness of speech as a sequence of phonemes arise spontaneously? *Cognition, 7,* 323–331.

Parker, F., & Riley, K. (1994). *Linguistics for non-linguists: A primer with exercises* (2nd ed.). Needham, MA: Allyn & Bacon.

Stanovich, K.E. (1986). Matthew effects in reading: Some consequences of individual differences in the acquisition of literacy. *Reading Research Quarterly, 21,* 360–406.

Treiman, R. (1993). Beginning to spell: A study of first grade children. New York: Oxford University Press.

Tunmer, W.E., & Nesdale, A.R. (1985). Phonemic segmentation skill and beginning reading. *Journal of Educational Psychology, 77,* 417–427.

Wagner, R., Torgesen, J.K., & Rashotte, C.A. (1994). Development of reading-related phonological processing abilities: New evidence of bidirectional causality from a latent variable longitudinal study. *Developmental Psychology, 30,* 73–87.

Wallach, L., Wallach, M.A., Dozier, M.G., & Kaplan, N.E. (1977). Poor children learning to read do not have trouble with auditory discrimination but do have trouble with phoneme recognition. *Journal of Educational Psychology, 69,* 36–39.

Wallach, M.A., & Wallach, L. (1979). Helping disadvantaged children learn to read by teaching them phoneme identification skills. In L.A. Resnick & P.A. Weaver (Eds.), *Theory and practice of early reading* (Vol. 3, pp. 227–259). Hillsdale, NJ: Lawrence Erlbaum Associates.

Williams, J.P. (1980). Teaching decoding with a special emphasis on phoneme analysis and phoneme blending. *Journal of Educational Psychology, 72,* 1–15.

2   The Language Games

By the time children enter kindergarten, their linguistic abilities are generally quite well developed. Their pronunciation is, for the most part, correct; their grammar is remarkably sophisticated; and they usually have little problem communicating with those around them.

In their natural, everyday communications, children usually concentrate on the meaning and message of what is being said. Yet, language also has another side to it: namely, its form and structure. Shifting attention from the meaning of language to its form is often very difficult for children at this age or stage of development. Therefore, despite their impressive abilities to speak and listen, they generally lack any conscious, reflective awareness of a language's parts or of how those parts combine and layer themselves in productive language.

Children in kindergarten and the first grade are the ideal age for learning to read and write. Yet, making sense of the mapping between written and spoken language depends on explicit knowledge of sentences, words, and phonemes because written language is explicitly organized into these units.

The goal of this program is to develop children's linguistic awareness—and, in particular, their phonemic awareness—in a way that cognitively prepares them for learning to read and write. The activities that follow in the next several chapters were originally developed for use with kindergarten children. Given only minor adjustments for pace and complexity, however, they can also be used in first-grade and special education settings (see Appendix C).

ABOUT THE USE OF THE LANGUAGE GAMES

For children to gain the most benefit from these goal-oriented games, it is important to stick to certain "rules."

1. You must play regularly—ideally, every day for about 15–20 minutes.
2. The games are sequenced according to difficulty. Although you may want to skip some games or add others, the overall sequence of objectives should be maintained. Once introduced, the games can be revisited in any order as often as needed or desired.

Suggested schedules for moving through the activities are provided in Appendices B and C. Bear in mind that these schedules are offered only as suggestions and should be adapted in both pace and complexity to best meet the range of needs and progress of the children in each classroom.

3. Prior to beginning the program, read the entire curriculum and become familiar with all of the activities. If you think your students are ready, you may wish to introduce an activity earlier than suggested in the schedule. For example, Activity 6A: Clapping Names is one with which many kindergarten children can be successful fairly early in the year, well before they are ready to do some of the other, more complex syllable-related activities. Even so, we caution against introducing this activity without first giving the children at least some groundwork in the concepts of words and sentences (Chapter 5).

4. In working with syllables and phonemes, it is important to regularly include activities involving both analysis and synthesis. *Analysis* refers to the breaking apart or segmentation of spoken words into syllables or phonemes. *Synthesis* refers to the blending of the syllables or phonemes into well-integrated spoken words. Both abilities are critical if children are to learn how the letters and spellings of written words map onto units of sound in spoken words. This mapping process is key to learning how to decode printed words when reading and how to encode spoken words when spelling.

5. While the designs of the games in this program are intended to have a lot of "child appeal," they are also instructionally effective. That is, the children should feel as though they are playing even while they are learning. Nevertheless, the expectation should not be that all of the children will immediately be successful with each activity. If this were the case, there would be no reason for the training.

Research shows that some children, by nature, find these sorts of language activities much easier than do others. You should expect a considerable span of abilities, ranging from great ease to intense difficulty, across your students; be prepared to deal with this range constructively. Toward this end, great care should be given to the way in which activities are presented so that no child feels either unsuccessful or restless.

One way to maintain an appropriate level of challenge across students is to vary the complexity of the materials used in each game. By extension, when calling on individual students, rather than the whole group, for a response, choose a child for whom the difficulty of the challenge is neither too hard nor too easy. By varying the complexity of the challenges and strategically choosing particular children for responses, you can find a way to make each feel good about her or his performance even as you collect information about each child's individual progress.

In similar spirit, as suggested in the schedule, new games should be introduced even as familiar ones or their variations are revisited. This helps to ensure that each session will include a productive mix of new and review. To this end, Advanced Language Games are presented in Appendix E. Finally, you should create extra time to work with those who need still more practice. One way to do this is by developing your students' ability to play games among themselves in small groups; games that are especially suited for small-group play are noted throughout the activities.

As a creative teacher, you will begin to have many ideas for new variations of the games that will enhance their value and make them more appealing to the children. As you develop your own ideas and variations, always be careful that the objective of the original activity remains intact.

Remember: Children do not pay attention when they are bored or frustrated, and they do not learn when they are not paying attention.

6. Remember throughout that the principal goal of this program is to lead the children to attend to the phonological aspects of speech and, ultimately, to help them to hear and feel the phonemes in words. You should consistently pronounce words and sounds very clearly and slowly and then ask the children to articulate these words and sounds aloud to ensure that they understand what is in reference.

Note, too, that those of us who already know how to read and write harbor a number of illusions about speech as a consequence. For example, your intuitions may tell you that the words of normal speech are separated by brief pauses, but that's not true; it's only your literate imagination tricking you. In fluent speech, the words run continuously, seamlessly, one into the next. Similarly, you should take care not to let your knowledge of spellings delude you about how various words sound; for example, *pitch* really does rhyme with *rich*—the /t/ is superfluous.

This is not a phonics program; it is a program that is supposed to make the logic of phonics self-evident when, later, it is taught. Thus, when adding print to an activity, do so only in support of the activity's phonological goals. Do not allow yourself to fall into the trap of distorting your pronunciations of sounds and words in deference to letter-names or spellings. We adults may find it awkward to focus on the sound as opposed to the spelling and the meaning of a word, but with practice the process becomes like second nature.

OVERVIEW OF THE PROGRAM

Each chapter is designed to develop a particular dimension of linguistic awareness, and each is designed to lay the groundwork for the next. Within chapters, too, the games are sequenced in order of the complexity or sophistication of their demands. The chapters, by title, and their major objectives are as follows:

- **Listening Games** To sharpen children's ability to attend selectively to sounds

- **Rhyming** To use rhyme to introduce the children to the sounds of words
- **Words and Sentences** To develop children's awareness that language is made up of strings of words
- **Awareness of Syllables** To develop the ability to analyze words into separate syllables and to develop the ability to synthesize words from a string of separate syllables
- **Initial and Final Sounds** To show the children that words contain phonemes and to introduce them to how phonemes sound and feel when spoken in isolation
- **Phonemes** To develop the ability to analyze words into a sequence of separate phonemes and to develop the ability to synthesize words from a sequence of separate phonemes
- **Introducing Letters and Spellings** To introduce the relation of letters to speech sounds
- **Assessing Phonological Awareness** To assess your children's general level of phonological awareness. The assessment procedure is designed for a group administration of up to 15 children at once with the supervision of two teachers. The assessment consists of six subtests, each containing five items: 1) Detecting Rhymes, 2) Counting Syllables, 3) Matching Initial Sounds, 4) Counting Phonemes, 5) Comparing Word Lengths, and 6) Representing Phonemes with Letters.

Exact instructions for each subtest are provided in Chapter 10, as well as line drawings of the pictures for limited reproduction by the teacher. Because the number of items per subtest is limited to five, reliability of scores for any one subtest is weak. The test is, therefore, not adequate by itself for identifying children who are at risk. Your students' average performance on these materials, however, can help you determine how much time—or how much more time—to spend on each chapter.

BRIEF DESCRIPTION OF THE GAMES IN PRACTICE

Chapter 3: Listening Games

The first set of activities has two purposes: The first purpose is to familiarize the children with the basic terms and dynamics of the activities before moving them into the more difficult language games that follow; the second purpose is to introduce them to the challenge of listening attentively. In the initial games, the children are asked to identify and sequence many everyday sounds, such as the wind, voices coming from other classes, the sound of scissors cutting, and so on. After that, they are moved into activities, such as following oral instructions, that require them to attend carefully to language.

Chapter 4: Rhyming

As rhyme play directs children's attention to the sound-structure of words, it seeds their awareness that language has not only meaning and message but also form. In addition to presenting a variety of rhyming games, we have included a list of sources for poems and rhyming stories (see Appendix F). Later in the year, enlarged text versions of these poems and stories can be revisited with the children for purposes of exploring print. In doing so, however, resist the temptation to direct their attention to complex (e.g., *light*) or incompatible (e.g., *word-bird*) spelling patterns—doing so at this point may confuse their budding sense of how the alphabet works.

Chapter 5: Words and Sentences

The games in this chapter should be played until all the children understand that language consists of sentences of different lengths and that these sentences, in turn, consist of words that also are of different lengths. This is the first step on the road to discovering that oral language is made up of layers of smaller and smaller linguistic units. Suggestions for adding print to these activities are included in the specific descriptions of each activity.

Chapter 6: Awareness of Syllables

In the syllables chapter, we go one step further, leading the children to discover that some words can be divided into smaller bits, namely syllables. The children start by clapping their own names and move on to clapping out the syllables of all different words, for example, *broccoli* becomes *broc-co-li* (analysis). They then advance to creating words from separate syllables; for instance, *broc-co-li* becomes *broccoli* (synthesis, which is more difficult). Throughout these games, it is important to pronounce the syllables clearly but without distorting them to capture details of the spellings.

Chapter 7: Initial and Final Sounds

Here, the children are led to concentrate on the first phoneme in a word and to discover how it sounds and feels when spoken in isolation; for instance, the word *nose* becomes *n-ose*. The children learn to make new words by taking an initial sound away; for instance, the word *sand* becomes *and* when we take away /s/ (analysis). In turn, the children are led to create new words by putting a sound in front of a word; as an example, /m/ in front of *ash* becomes *mash* (synthesis). After establishing these insights with initial sounds of words, the children's attention is turned to the final sounds of words. These activities tend to be difficult for some children, and it may take quite a while before all catch on.

Chapter 8: Phonemes

Not until all of these lessons are understood do we go on to divide words into single sounds (i.e., phonemes). For instance, the word *me* becomes /m/-/e/. To make these concepts as concrete as possible for the children, we recommend the use of colored blocks, cubes, animal counters, chips, or any other type of physical counter to represent the separate sounds of the words in sequence. Remember always to arrange the blocks from left to right so that the reading direction is incorporated into the games from the beginning.

The children are also encouraged to feel their own mouths while they articulate so that they will become aware of the differences in the position of the mouth when they pronounce different phonemes. It is also a good idea to encourage them to observe the teacher's mouth or to look at each other's mouths while articulating the phonemes.

Chapter 9: Introducing Letters and Spellings

Once children are able to divide words into single-speech sounds, they are ready to learn how to map the sounds onto letters. In fact, letters can make the phonemes easier to learn as they offer names and visual symbols to anchor their respective identities. Importantly, the goal of the letter-sound activities in Chapter 9 is only to lead the children to understand the basic alphabetic principle: that the letters in a written word, left to right, represent the sequence of phonemes in a spoken word, first to last. Only letter-sound and spelling-sound patterns that support that principle are explored.

3   Listening Games

Hearing nonspeech sounds is relatively easy and natural for people—provided that they pay attention. Therein lies the primary motive for these initial listening games: to introduce the children to the art of listening actively, attentively, and analytically.

The children are asked to listen to many everyday sounds, such as the rush of the wind, the hum of an air conditioner, and the snipping of scissors. With closed eyes, they are asked to identify the sounds, to remember their order, and to locate their sources. Once the nature of the game has been established, the children are given similar activities with meaningful language in place of environmental sounds. For example, they are asked to listen to poems and stories that are very familiar, except that, every now and then, the familiar wordings have been replaced with nonsense. In detecting such changes, the children are learning to listen—not for what they expect, but for what they actually hear. In this way, they are introduced to the art of listening actively, attentively, and analytically.

3A Listening to Sounds

Objective To allow children to explore their listening powers and to practice focusing their attention on particular sounds of interest

Materials needed Tape recording of various sounds (optional)
Tape player (optional)

Activity Our world is filled with sounds. Through this game, the children will discover that, if they listen, they can hear sounds from outdoors, indoors, and even from within themselves. Before starting the game, talk about the difference between listening with closed eyes and with open eyes. Then ask the children to sit with closed eyes and just listen for a few moments. After a few minutes, invite them to name different sounds that they hear. The children will quickly learn to listen actively. Sounds that may be heard include the following:

birds	drips	rustling of treetops
breathing	fan	swallowing
cars	flies	trucks
clocks	footsteps	voices
dogs	heartbeat	wind blowing

Variation • For variety or to extend the range of sounds that can be heard, repeat this game in a different location or using tape recordings.

NOTES AND ADDITIONAL ACTIVITIES

3B   Listening to Sequences of Sounds

Objective

To develop the memory and attentional abilities for thinking about sequences of sounds and the language for discussing them

Materials needed

Objects that make interesting, distinctive sounds. Some examples follow:

banging on wall/table/lap	opening window or drawer
blowing	pouring liquid
blowing a whistle	ringing a bell
blowing nose	rubbing hands together
clapping	scratching
clicking with tongue	sharpening a pencil
closing purse	slamming a book
coloring hard on paper	smashing crackers
coughing	snapping fingers
crumpling paper	stamping
cutting with a knife	stirring with teaspoon
cutting with scissors	tearing paper
dropping (various things)	tiptoeing
drumming with fingers	turning on computer
eating an apple	walking
folding paper	whistling
hammering	writing on board
hopping	writing with a pencil
noisy chewing	

Activity

In this game, the children are challenged first to identify single sounds and then to identify each one of a sequence of sounds. Both will be very important in the language games to come. The children are to cover their eyes with their hands while you make a familiar noise such as closing the door, sneezing, or playing a key on the piano. By listening carefully and without peeking, the children are to try to identify the noise.

Once the children have caught on to the game, make two noises, one after the other. Without peeking, the children are to guess the two sounds in sequence saying, "There were two sounds. First we heard a _____, and then we heard a _____."

After the children have become quite good with pairs of noises, produce series of more than two for them to identify and report in sequence. Again, complete sentences should be encouraged.

Remember that, to give every child the opportunity to participate mentally in these games, it is important to discourage all children from calling out their answers until they are asked to do so. In addition, both to support full participation and to allow assessment of individual students, it is helpful to switch unpredictably between inviting a response from the whole group and from individual children of your designation.

Note: Because of the importance of the skill exercised through this game, invest special care in noting every child's progress and difficulties. Extra opportunities should be created to work with children who are having trouble with the concept of sequences or in expressing their responses.

Variations

- With the children's eyes closed, make a series of sounds. Then repeat the sequence, but omit one of the sounds. The children must identify the sound that has been omitted from the second sequence.

- Invite the children to make sounds for their classmates to guess.

- These games also offer good opportunities to review, exercise, and evaluate children's use of ordinal terms such as first, second, third, middle, last. It is worth ensuring that every student gains comfortable, receptive, and expressive command of these terms.

NOTES AND ADDITIONAL ACTIVITIES

3C Jacob, Where Are You?

Objective   To encourage children's willingness to listen sensitively and thoughtfully

Activity   Whereas the prior games were designed to develop the children's ability to listen selectively, this one is intended to help children locate the source of a sound by listening only. Encourage the children to sit quietly in a circle. One child, with eyes covered, should be seated in the center of the circle (or lying down, "sleeping"). Meanwhile, another child is asked to play the part of "Jacob." "Jacob" goes to any part of the room and makes an animal sound (e.g., "moo," "bow-wow," "peep," "bzzzz"). The child in the center of the circle must try to point to "Jacob." In addition, she or he must try to name the part of the room to which "Jacob" has gone and to indicate whether "Jacob" is, for example, lying down on the floor or standing on a chair. The goal is to pinpoint from where in the room the sound is coming.

When the child in the middle of the circle has figured out from where the sound is coming, the child who was hiding goes into the middle and a new "Jacob" is chosen.

Variation   • Children may use sounds other than animal sounds, perhaps sounds tied to a particular theme being studied in the classroom.

NOTES AND ADDITIONAL ACTIVITIES

3D 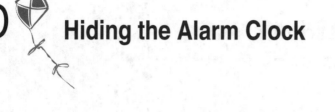 Hiding the Alarm Clock

Objective

To locate a sound that, moment by moment, blends easily with the random noises in the environment—to successfully locate it, the children must develop and expand upon the ability to stretch their listening attention in time

Materials needed

Ticking clock or timer

Activity

Ask one of the children to cover her or his eyes. While the child's eyes are covered, hide a ticking clock or timer. The child then uncovers her or his eyes and tries to find the ticking clock by listening. During the search, all the other children must be as quiet as mice, trying not to give away any hints.

NOTES AND ADDITIONAL ACTIVITIES

3E   **Who Says What?**

Objective   To listen for a particular sound and to pair it with its source

Materials needed   An assortment of toy animals or pictures of animals
Storybook (optional)

Activity   In this activity, the sounds are animal noises and the sources are the animals that make those noises. Later, the game will be played with phonemes and letters. Distribute toy animals or pictures of animals to the children and ask, "What kind of animal (roars, meows, peeps, etc.)?" The child with the matching toy or picture is to hold it up for all to see while responding, "It is a (lion) that (roars)." It is worth including a figure or picture of a human and to ask, "What kind of animal talks?"

Note: Most children will find this activity quite easy. This makes it ideal for sandwiching among more difficult activities, because all children should feel successful in some activity every day. Because it is so easy, however, the children will tire of it quickly unless it is varied.

Variation
- Find a children's storybook that has animal characters matching the toy animals you have already distributed to the children. Whenever the name of an animal is mentioned in the text, substitute the sound that animal makes for its name. The child or children who have the corresponding animal figure should hold it up.

3F Whisper Your Name

Objective

For children to pick out one specific sound from many similar sounds that are heard at once

Materials needed

Blindfold

Activity

Take one child (the "listening child") and move to another part of the room where, together, you can secretly select the name of some other child in the classroom. Then blindfold the child.

Meanwhile, all of the other children are standing in a circle, whispering their own names. The "listening child" is guided around the circle by the adult, listening for the name that was selected. On hearing the selected name, the "listening child" embraces its speaker.

NOTES AND ADDITIONAL ACTIVITIES

3G Nonsense

Objective

To develop the children's ability to attend to differences between what they expect to hear and what they actually hear

Materials needed

Book of familiar stories or poems

Activity

Invite the children to sit down and close their eyes so that they can concentrate on what they will hear. Then recite or read aloud a familiar story or poem to the children but, once in a while, by changing its words or wording, change its sense to nonsense. The children's challenge is to detect such changes whenever they occur. When they do, encourage them to explain what was wrong. As the game is replayed in more subtle variations across the year, it will also serve usefully to sharpen the children's awareness of the phonology, words, syntax, and semantics of language.

As illustrated in the following list, you can change any text in more or less subtle ways at a number of different levels including phonemes, words, grammar, and meaning. Because of this, the game can be profitably and enjoyably revisited again and again throughout the year. Even so, in initial plays of the game, it is important that the changes result in violations of the sense, meaning, and wording of the text that are relatively obvious. Following are some examples of the "nonsense" that can be created within familiar poems and rhymes:

Song a sing of sixpence	Reverse words
Baa baa purple sheep	Substitute words
Twinkle, twinkle little car	Substitute words
Humpty Dumpty wall on a sat	Swap word order (ungrammatical)
Jack fell down and crown his broke	Swap word order (ungrammatical)
One, two, shuckle my boo	Swap word parts
I'm a tittle leapot	Swap word parts
The eensy weensy spider went up the spouter wat.	Swap word parts
One, two, buckle my shoe Five, six, pick up sticks	Switch order of events (grammatical)

Little Miss Muffet, eating a tuffet	
Sat on her curds and whey	Switch order of events (grammatical)
Goldilocks went inside and knocked	
on the door.	Switch order of events (grammatical)
The first little piggy built himself a house	
of bricks.	Switch order of events (grammatical)

Note: Don't forget to switch unpredictably between asking the whole group or individual children to respond.

NOTES AND ADDITIONAL ACTIVITIES

3H Whispering Game

Objective   To exercise the children's ability to overcome distractions, pronunciation differences, and so on, while listening to language

Activity   Seat the children in a circle. Then whisper something to the child on your left; that child then whispers something to the child on her or his left, and so on. The whispering continues, child to child, in clockwise order until it reaches the last child, who says out loud whatever she or he has heard.

　　We add that this game is difficult for a variety of reasons. The youngest children may need preliminary practice in passing to the left; this can be done by asking them to tap each other in turn or to pass an object from one to the next. To make the game linguistically easier, try putting children in small groups of no more than five initially. Begin with single words, then go to phrases, and then to full sentences only as children develop skill (and maturity).

Note: You may want to position yourself next to children with limited English proficiency in order to help them understand the message and effectively pass it to the next child. If there are many children in the classroom who have speech problems or limited English proficiency and diverse language backgrounds, the game is best skipped.

NOTES AND ADDITIONAL ACTIVITIES

31   Do You Remember?

Objective

To exercise children's ability to remember and execute actions in sequential steps and, more generally, to develop the kind of attentive listening that is necessary for understanding and following verbal instructions (both are extremely important abilities for the young student)

Materials needed

Picture cards (optional)

Activity

This is a game of sequential instructions. Instruct the child who is "it" to complete a series of actions (e.g., "Stand up, lift one leg, hop to the door, and say *boo*!"). Meanwhile, the rest of the children are to listen and watch carefully, giving a thumbs-up or thumbs-down depending on whether the first child follows the instructions correctly (i.e., executes the correct actions in the correct order).

    The first several times this game is played, the instructions should be kept relatively simple and short. With revisits and depending on the capabilities of the particular child who is "it," their length and syntactic complexity should be increased to maintain the appropriate level of challenge and instructional benefit. In particular, this game and its variations offer special opportunity for developing the children's awareness and understanding of prepositions and relational words such as *over, under, behind, before, after, in front of, middle, last, while, until*. Following are examples:

1. Easy: "Go to the table. Pick up the book."
2. Harder: "Crawl under the table. Stand up. Pick up three books. Smile."
3. Hard: "Stand on your right foot. Take four hops to the table. Pick up two books while you smile at Rosa."

Note: Observe the children carefully to determine who may need extra support and practice.

Variations

- Ask a child to give the instructions to another child. To increase involvement, you may wish to divide the children into groups of five or so.

- Early on or with younger children, it may be helpful to use action picture cards in addition to the oral directions.

- Once the children are comfortable with the basic game, playing Simon Says with the whole class can be a fun and powerful means of exercising and extending these sorts of language and listening skills.

NOTES AND ADDITIONAL ACTIVITIES

4  Rhyming

Sensitivity to rhyme comes quite easily to most children. For that reason, rhyme play is an excellent entry to phonological awareness. Because rhyme play directs children's attention to similarities and differences in the sounds of words, it is a useful means of alerting them to the insight that language has not only meaning and message but also physical form.

Through the activities in this section, the children are invited to attend to and play with rhymes in many different ways. They are asked to listen to rhyming stories, to recite rhyming songs and poems, to use meaning and meter to help anticipate specific rhyming words as they listen, and to generate rhymes on their own. Remember that the purpose of these lessons is to develop the children's attention to the sounds of language. With that in mind, there is no need to divert attention to the spellings of words; in fact, unless the rhyming words are similarly spelled, it may even be confusing to do so.

Again, sensitivity to rhyme is a very rudimentary form of phonological awareness. Yet, having a solid command of rhyming is no guarantee that a child will develop phonemic awareness. However, research does affirm that it is a valuable step in the right direction.

4A Poetry, Songs, and Jingles

Objective

To use poems and chants in ways that enhance children's awareness of the sound patterns of speech

Materials needed

Book of rhyming poems, songs, or jingles

Activity

Rhyming poems, songs, and jingles that children have learned by heart offer special opportunities for rhyme play. For your convenience, a number of learnable poems, fingerplays, jingles, and chants are suggested in Appendix G. Initially, introduce children to only one or two rhymes that they can learn well. More rhymes can always be added to their repertoire in time.

In introducing a new poem or chant, first read or recite it for the children, emphasizing its rhythm and exaggerating its rhymes. Then, rereading line by line, the children should repeat each line in unison. So that all can hear and learn the words, the pace should be slow and deliberate at first, gradually picking up speed as the children gain mastery.

Variations

- Recite the poem in whispers, but say the rhyming words aloud.

- Recite the poem in very loud voices, but whisper the rhyming words.

- Recite the poem in crescendoing voices, getting louder and louder as you go.

- Recite the poem in decrescendoing voices, getting softer and softer as you go.

- Recite the poem in a canon or round.

- Seat the children in a circle, and ask them to recite successive lines of the poem, one at a time, in turn.

- Seat the children in a circle, and ask them to recite successive words of the poem, one at a time, in turn.

4B   Rhyme Stories

Objective   To teach the children to use meaning and meter to notice and predict rhyming words

Materials needed   Rhyming book

Activity   By their very structure, rhyme stories invite students to use meaning and meter to notice and predict rhyming words. An annotated bibliography of suggested books and stories is provided in Appendix F. While reading such stories aloud, exaggerate the meter and rhyme to encourage active listening and anticipation among the children.

In the course of reading the first story with the children, take an opportunity to anchor students' understanding of the words *rhyme* and *rhyming*. Prior to reading subsequent stories, check for an understanding of what rhyming is and remind the children to listen for words that rhyme.

Variations
- When reading a book that is already familiar to children, stop after rhyming words and ask them what words they heard that rhyme.

- Alternatively, stop before reading the second word of a rhyming pair, and ask the children to guess the word before you continue.

NOTES AND ADDITIONAL ACTIVITIES

4C   Emphasizing Rhyme Through Movement

Objective   To focus children's attention on rhyme

Activity   Multisensory play is, in general, a valuable means of capturing young children's attention. The traditional children's rhyme, "One Potato, Two Potato, Three Potato, Four," offers an excellent framework for tying physical movement to rhyme. The children are to sit in a circle with both fists before them. While all the children chant the rhyme, the person who is "it" moves around the circle and (gently) pounds out the stressed syllables, first on the right fist then on the left fist of each child. A child whose fist is pounded on the last or rhyming word of each line (i.e., on one of the "magic" words) must put that fist behind her or his back. As soon as any child loses both hands, she or he is out. The last child remaining with one fist still in front becomes the new "it." In "One Potato, Two Potato," the stressed syllables are the number words:

> **"One** potato, **two** potato, **three** potato, **four"**
> **"Five** potato, **six** potato, **seven** potato, **more"**

Variation

- It is useful to extend this game to other rhymes as well. Suggestions include the following:

"Eeny Meeny Miney Mo"	Magic words: Mo, toe, go, Mo
"Pease Porridge Hot"	Magic words: cold, old, hot, pot
"Hickory, Dickory Dock"	Magic words: dock, clock
"Baa, Baa Black Sheep"	Magic words: wool, full
"One, Two, Buckle My Shoe"	Magic words: two, shoe; four, door; and so forth

4D ⬦ Word Rhyming

Objective

To evoke the realization that almost any word can be rhymed—not just those in other people's poems

Materials needed

List of words to be rhymed

Activity

In this game, you produce a word to be rhymed (e.g., *cat*), then signal to the children to give a rhyming word. You can increase the game's complexity by additionally challenging the children to suggest a second word that is meaningfully related to your clue word as well as a rhyme for that word. Once the game is familiar, individual children may be invited to respond and to choose the next word to be rhymed. Examples include the following:

cat–hat	dog–?
car–far	truck–?
mouse–house	rat–?
bag–rag	sack–?
chair–hair	sota–?
talk–walk	shout–?
rose–hose	flower–?
book–hook	read–?
face–lace	smile–?
bed–red	night–?

Note: Do not expect children to play this game as an adult would. Many of their rhymes will be nonsense words, which is fine because the purpose of exercising rhymes in the first place is to cause them to attend to the sounds of language. Similarly, many of their associative responses may seem, at best, barely related to the clue word; again, this is fine. The purpose of the game is to demonstrate that almost any word can be rhymed.

4E  Can You Rhyme?

Objective To teach children to depend more strongly on phonological cues to generate rhymes

Materials needed Sample rhyme phrases

Activity To introduce this game, read several rhyme phrases aloud, emphasizing the rhyming words. Then, challenge the children to complete each rhyme aloud. For assessment purposes, it is recommended that you periodically request responses from individuals as opposed to the whole group. Following are examples of phrases that can be used:

A **cat** wearing a _____(hat).
A **mouse** that lives in a _____(house).
A **moose** with a tooth that is _____(loose).
A **pig** that is dancing a _____(jig).
Some **kittens** wearing some _____(mittens).
A **sheep** that is sound _____(asleep).
An **owl** drying off with a _____(towel).
A **bear** with long, brown _____(hair).
A **bug** crawled under the _____(rug).
An **ape** that is eating a _____(grape).
A **goat** that is sailing a _____(boat).
A **duck** that is driving a _____(truck).
A **guy** who is swatting a _____(fly).
A **bee** with a hive in the _____(tree).
On the **swing**, I like to _____(sing).
We drove **far** in our _____(car).
Hold the **candle** by the _____(handle).
Smell the **rose** with your _____(nose).
Write the numbers one to **ten** with a pencil or a _____(pen).
Dancing, dancing, cross the **floor,** keep on dancing out the _____(door).
Airplanes **fly** up in the _____(sky).

Variations

- Early in the year, as children are learning to rhyme, try inventing new rhymes and singing them to the tune of "If You're Happy and You Know It" as follows:

  > Did you ever see a (bear) in a (chair)?
  > Did you ever see a (bear) in a (chair) ?
  > No, I never, no, I never, no, I never, no, I never
  > No, I never saw a (bear) in a (chair).

- Later in the year, after the children have had lots of practice with rhymes, they may enjoy singing "Down by the Bay." The fun of the song is that children must supply a rhyming phrase (e.g., a mouse painting a house, a bird spelling a word, a fly wearing a tie) for the next-to-last line.

  > Down by the bay
  > Where the watermelons grow.
  > That's where I know,
  > I dare not go.
  > For if I do,
  > My mother will say,
  > "Did you ever see a (goose kissing a moose)?"
  > Down by the bay!

NOTES AND ADDITIONAL ACTIVITIES

4F 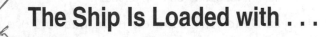 The Ship Is Loaded with . . .

Objective   To teach children to respond quickly without any context clues

Materials needed   Something to toss (ball or beanbag)

Activity   Seat the children in a circle, and make sure you have something to toss, such as a ball or a beanbag. To begin the game, say, "The ship is loaded with *cheese*." Then toss the ball to somebody in the circle. This person must produce a rhyme (e.g., "The ship is loaded with *peas*") and throw the ball back to you. Repeating your original rhyme, then toss the ball to another child. Continue the game in this way until the children run out of rhymes. Then begin the game again with new cargo.

When the children have become good at rhyming, each child can throw the ball to another child instead of back to you. The second child must then continue rhyming on the word suggested by the first child.

The ship is loaded with *cheese*.	(peas, fleas, trees, bees, keys, etc.)
The ship is loaded with *logs*.	(dogs, hogs, frogs, etc.)
The ship is loaded with *mats*.	(cats, rats, bats, hats, etc.)
The ship is loaded with *stars*.	(cars, bars, jars, cigars, etc.)

Note: The pace needs to move quickly or children will lose interest while waiting their turn. If necessary, review possible rhyme families with the children prior to beginning the game.

NOTES AND ADDITIONAL ACTIVITIES

4G Action Rhymes

Objective   To expose the children to a new level of phonological awareness in which they attend to word stems

Materials needed   Pictures of rhyming word pairs

Activity   This game, which encourages children to push through the -ing suffix and attend to word stems, is best introduced to the children in small groups because it is complex in both its rhyming and sentence-formation demands. You should distribute the pictures corresponding to one of each rhyming pair to the students, keeping its mate yourself. To explain how the game is played, show your picture and say a sentence using the depicted action word (e.g., "The bell is *ringing*"). Then ask the students to examine their own cards to see if they show an action that rhymes with ringing. If so, the child is to hold up the card and make a rhyming sentence (e.g., "The children are *singing*"). Once the game has been familiarized in small groups, the whole class can play together. Following are examples of action rhymes:

barking–parking	mixing–fixing
burning–turning	neighing–playing
creeping–sleeping	riding–hiding
cutting–shutting	ringing–singing
dining–shining	sewing–rowing
draining–raining	singing–ringing
fighting–writing	skipping–ripping
freezing–sneezing	speaking–leaking
frying–crying	spinning–winning
heating–eating	talking–walking
hopping–mopping	thinking–drinking
jumping–dumping	weeding–reading
knitting–sitting	wishing–fishing
looking–cooking	

4H Rhyme Book

Objective To celebrate and exhibit the children's mastery of rhyme

Materials needed
Paper
Crayons
Markers
Pictures
Glue

Activity Creating a rhyme book is an excellent way to celebrate and show off the children's mastery of rhyme. Once the children are quite good at rhyming, they will find it rewarding to make a rhyme book. Conferring with each other as needed, each child should make up a rhyming couplet that you will write for each child. The child can then add an illustration. A few children can be invited to share their pages with the class each day until all have participated. The pages may then be collected and displayed or published as a book.

NOTES AND ADDITIONAL ACTIVITIES

5   Words and Sentences

Because the goal of this book is to lead students to think about the structure of language in a way that affords them a productive understanding of the logic of our writing system, the activities in this chapter give the students a basic awareness of words and sentences. Although their appreciation of both sentences and words will continue to grow and change throughout their literary careers, the activities in this chapter seek only to establish basic and essential starting points.

True appreciation of the syntax and constraints that give sentences their clarity and cohesion can only be developed over time. Furthermore, this appreciation is, to a significant extent, learnable and worth learning only through real reading and writing experiences. The goals of this chapter are to alert children to three basic properties of sentences:

1. Sentences are the linguistic packages through which we convey our separate thoughts.
2. Sentences are, in turn, composed of strings of separately speakable, meaningful words.
3. The meaning or meaningfulness of a sentence depends on the particular words it contains as well as on the specific order of words.

Without argument, learning how to read or write depends on a relatively secure notion of what is and is not a word. Yet, research affirms that young children generally possess only the vaguest awareness of words and their nature. In view of this, a major focus of this chapter is directed to clarifying children's concepts of words. Several of the games are designed to develop the children's ability to analyze sentences into their separate words. In addition, the children are led to notice that they can think about the form of a word independently of its meaning through a game in which they judge the lengths of different words.

5A Introducing the Idea of Sentences

Objective

To introduce the children to the notion of sentences

Materials needed

Pictures (optional)

Activity

Begin by presenting the children with a simple explanation of a sentence. For example, explain that a sentence is like a very short story. And just like a story, a sentence has to tell something and has to name who or what it is telling about.

You can then give some examples of sentences using the names of your students as subjects (e.g., "Pam has a school bag," "Morton has new boots," "Kate is wearing a red shirt"). After each example, repeat that this is a sentence, and the children are to repeat the word "sentence" loudly in unison. To clarify, you should also give some sentences without subjects (e.g., "has brown eyes," "is wearing pink socks"). After asking if each is a sentence, explain that such phrases cannot be sentences because a sentence must name who or what it is about. Then complete the sentence (e.g., "Calvin's mother has brown eyes," "Regina is wearing pink socks").

Similarly, to show that a sentence needs a predicate, ask whether the following are sentences: "the children," "Jocelyn." Then explain that these cannot be sentences because, even though we know who they are about, they do not tell us anything about them. After sharing a few such examples, invite three or four children to share their own sentences.

Although this is enough for the first day, this activity should be revisited until all the children can comfortably produce a sentence. In addition, encourage the children, with sensitive restraint, to use complete sentences throughout each school day.

Variations

- Ask the students to develop sentences about a picture shown. By using a complex picture or mural, many different sentences are made possible.

- Ask children to judge your statements as sentences or nonsentences by "thumbs up" or "thumbs down." If they identify a nonsentence, encourage the children to complete the sentence or to describe why it is incomplete.

5B  Introducing the Idea of a Word

Objective

To introduce the children to the idea that sentences are made of strings of words

Materials needed

Word cards or flipcharts
Markers
Pens
Eraser board
Chalk
Chalkboard

Activity

Produce a sentence made of two monosyllabic words (e.g., "John eats"). Then explain to the children that the sentence has two parts, namely, two words. To represent the words concretely, build the sentence from separate word cards or write it on the board, drawing boxes around each word.

Then make a new three-word sentence (e.g., "Pat sits down"). The new sentence is placed or written right beneath the first sentence, as shown in the following example:

Discuss the number of words and compare the lengths of the two sentences, leading the children to conclude that the second sentence is the longest because it has the most words. To reinforce the point, explore several more sentences in this way.

Note: Take care to use only monosyllabic words until the children have learned to distinguish words from syllables.

Variations

- Challenge the children to tell you how many words are in each sentence before displaying it visually.

- Point out to the children that, in normal print, words are separated from one another by little blank spaces. As the year progresses, they should learn how to fingerpoint familiar text as you read it aloud to them.

- Using the word cards, demonstrate to the children how the sense or meaning of a sentence changes when the words are reordered.

NOTES AND ADDITIONAL ACTIVITIES

5C Hearing Words in Sentences

Objective

To strengthen the children's awareness of words by challenging them to represent each with a separate block

Materials needed

Blocks or squares of heavy paper

Activity

Give each child six or seven ordinary blocks, interlocking cubes, or squares of heavy paper, which they will use to represent the words in a sentence that you produce—one block for each word. Model the required thought process for the children, showing them how to repeat your sentences to themselves word by word with clear pauses between each. Also encourage the children to arrange the blocks from left to right so that they begin to establish directionality.

After arranging their blocks, the group or a designated individual should be asked to repeat your sentence, pointing to each block while pronouncing the word it represents. Then everyone repeats the sentence while pointing to each of their blocks.

At first, all sentences should be short (two or three words). Once the children have become comfortable with the activity, however, longer sentences should be introduced as the children should be led to observe that longer sentences have more words.

Again, care should be taken to use monosyllabic words until after they have completed the chapter on syllables. After the chapter on syllables and periodically throughout the year, this activity should be revisited as it will help children to reinforce their ability to distinguish syllables from words.

Variations

- Once more complex sentences and polysyllabic words are introduced, the students are likely to demonstrate difficulty in deciding whether such function words as *a, the, in, of, on, for, with, not,* and so forth should count as words in their own right. The development of syntactic awareness depends critically on an understanding of the function words. Yet, children have difficulty developing awareness of the function words. Toward establishing awareness of these ubiquitous words and supporting the children's syntactic development at the same time, find ways to play games such as Simon Says that put their usage in focus. For example, Simon says, "Put the pencil on top of the book." Note, too, that such games offer a good opportunity to build sight recognition as well as proper usage and understanding of these words.

NOTES AND ADDITIONAL ACTIVITIES

5D   Exercises with Short and Long Words

Objective

To refine the children's awareness of words per se and, more specifically, to help them realize that words are defined by meaning and that they can be long or short independently of their meaning

Materials needed

Chalk/chalkboard
Magnetic letters or word cards
Storybook (optional)

Activity

The major point of the preceding games is that sentences consist of nothing more or less than strings of words. To make this point as obviously and easily as possible, each of the games was to be played with monosyllabic words only. It is now time to disabuse the children of any notion that all words are exactly one syllable long.

The play of this game requires children to decide which of two words is phonologically longer. In making this judgment, children often have trouble separating form from meaning. Knowing that a ladybug is smaller than a cow, for example, they may resist agreeing that the word *ladybug* is longer than the word *cow*.

Therefore, the game has been designed in recognition of this tendency. Each pair of words includes one that is phonologically longer than the other. Independently of their lengths, one of the words refers to a familiar object that is significantly larger than the other. This design forces the children to dissociate form from meaning in judging the words' lengths. Also, it gives the teacher a way of detecting if they are not.

Because the written forms of the words are used as feedback for the children's judgments, it is important that they be printed in a way that makes the differences in their spelled lengths obvious. This can be accomplished in a number of ways. One is to emphasize the words' lengths in letters by spelling them with magnetic letters. Another is to preprint the words in large, uniform letters on rectangles of posterboard to allow emphasis of differences in their overall lengths. A third is to print the words above and beneath each other on the board, aligning their initial letters to make obvious their differences in length.

To play the game, pronounce a pair of words (e.g., *car* and *ambulance*) and ask the children which word they think is longer. When the children have answered, show them the words in print so that they can see if their judgments were correct. Useful pairs of words include the following:

ant–brontosaurus
bee–butterfly
bus–motorcycle
car–automobile
cow–ladybug
dog–giraffe
elephant–cat
mosquito–truck
tree–flower

Note: Remember that the objective is for children to learn to *hear* the differences in the lengths of the words. In support of this objective, the print should not be revealed until the children have judged "longer" or "shorter" through listening.

Variations

• Return to this game once the children have learned to analyze words into syllables. Invite them to clap the syllables of each word as a way of verifying which is longer and which is shorter. Then show the words in print as reinforcement.

• Pull words from stories you have shared with the children and ask which is longer or shorter. Then take children back to the original text to see the words in print.

• Ask the children to ask their parents to give them some very long words or names that they can share with their classmates.

• Read "Tikki Tikki Tembo" with the children.

NOTES AND ADDITIONAL ACTIVITIES

5E  Words in Context and Out

Objective

To solidify the point that a word is a word by itself or in context even as the meaning of language depends on its specific words and their order

Materials needed

A collection of rhymes or poems familiar to the children
Pocket charts (optional)
Word cards (optional)

Activity

For this game, every child is assigned one word of a familiar rhyme. By lining up properly and announcing their words in sequence, the whole rhyme can be recited. If the words are recited in any other order, the sentence changes or loses its meaning.

Pick a familiar rhyme that has roughly as many words as there are students in your class. "This Little Piggy Went to Market" will be used to illustrate the procedure. Recite the first line of the poem with the children and ask them to help you figure out how many words it has. Then choose the same number of children and assign one word of the sentence to each child: *This* to the first child, *little* to the second child, *piggy* to the third, and so forth. Have all six children stand up in a left-to-right line and ask each to say his or her word in order. Ask them to do this several times until they can produce the line with enough fluency that it is comprehensible.

Repeat the above for each successive line of the poem. After all lines have been assigned and practiced, ask the children to recite the rhyme all the way through, beginning with the first child in the first line and ending with the last child in the last line.

Variations

- Invite the children in a line to call out their words from right to left instead of from left to right.

- Invite the children in a line to scramble their order before calling out the words from left to right.

47

- Invite the children to make new lines of five or six children each, depending on, for example, the color of their clothes. Then ask each line to call out its words from left to right.

- Invite some particular group of children to leave their line (e.g., all the girls, all those wearing striped shirts, all those who have a pet cat). Ask the remainder to recite from left to right.

- Invite each line of children to explore among themselves what happens to their line of the poem when they exclude one or more person(s) or rearrange their order. Each group can be invited to share their favorite result along with the original line with the class.

Advanced Variation

- After the children have begun to move into print, all of these games are worth replaying either with pocket charts or by passing a printed word card to each child.

NOTES AND ADDITIONAL ACTIVITIES

6   Awareness of Syllables

Once the students have established that sentences are made of words, it is time to introduce them to the idea that words are, themselves, made of strings of still smaller units of speech—syllables.

Because, unlike words, syllables are meaningless, it is unlikely that the children have ever noticed or thought about them before. Yet, the successive syllables of spoken language can be both heard and felt: They correspond to the sound pulses of the voice as well as to the opening and closing cycles of the jaw. For these reasons, most children find the syllable games new and difficult enough to be interesting but easy enough to be completely feasible. Even so, because an awareness of syllables is an important step for developing a useful awareness of phonemes, the teacher should maintain a careful eye for any children who do experience difficulty, giving them extra help as needed.

The existence and nature of syllables is introduced by asking the children to clap and count the pulses of their own names. By extending this challenge to a variety of different words, the children's concept of the syllable is then strengthened and enriched; for example, *broccoli* becomes *broc-co-li*. The games then advance from analysis to synthesis as the children learn to put together or recognize words given sequences of their separate syllables: for example, *broc-co-li* once again becomes *broccoli*.

Before beginning the activities, some general advice is in order. First, care should be taken that all children are familiar with the words used in the games played, for it is very difficult to remember the sounds of an unfamiliar word. Second, throughout these games, the syllables should be enunciated clearly and distinctly. Third, the children should develop a level of comfort both in analyzing words into their separate syllables and in synthesizing words from their separate syllables. Although this chapter orders the games in a particular manner, the first few games focus on analysis and the last few on synthesis; all of the games can be used in any order on revisits.

6A  Clapping Names

Objective   To introduce the children to the nature of syllables by leading them to clap and count the syllables in their own names

Activity   When you first introduce this activity, model it by using several names of contrasting lengths. Pronounce the first name of one of the children in the classroom syllable by syllable while clapping it out before inviting the children to say and clap the name along with you. After each name has been clapped, ask "How many syllables did you hear?" Once the children have caught on, ask each child to clap and count the syllables in his or her own name. Don't forget last names, too! It is easy to continue clapping other words and to count the syllables in each. When doing the activity for the first time, model each child's name by pronouncing it, clapping it, and then having all of the children clap it together. After each name has been clapped by all of the children, ask "How many syllables did you hear?" If a name has many syllables, you may need to let children count the syllables as they are clapping.

Variations
- Ask the children to clap and count the syllables of their first and last names together.

- After determining the number of syllables in a name, ask the children to hold two fingers horizontally under their chins, so they can feel the chin drop for each syllable. To maximize this effect, encourage the children to elongate or stretch each syllable.

- As follows, this activity can be done to a rhythmic chant, such as "Bippity, Bippity Bumble Bee":

  Bippity, bippity bumble bee, tell me what your name should be.

  (Point to a child; that child responds by giving his name. Class repeats name out loud. Continue with one of the following:)
  1. "Clap it!" (Children repeat name, enunciating and clapping to each syllable.)
  2. "Whisper it!" (Children whisper each syllable while clapping.)
  3. "Silent!" (Children repeat name, silently enunciating syllables with mouth movement.)

6B  Take One Thing from the Box

Objective   To reinforce the children's ability to analyze words into syllables by asking them to clap and count the syllables in a variety of different words

**Materials
Needed**   A box of small objects
Pictures of various objects (optional)

Activity   Collect a number of objects in a box or basket. Make sure to include
objects that differ from one another in the number of syllables in their
name.

Invite one student to close her or his eyes, choose an object from the
container, and name it (e.g., "This is a pencil"). All of the children should
repeat the chosen object's name as they clap out its syllables. Then ask
how many syllables were heard, taking care not to let anyone call out the
answer too soon.

Gradually, as the children get better at the game, you can make it
more difficult by using items with names that are longer and collectively
more varied in length. Happily, children tend to find very long words delightfully amusing.

Variations   • Use physical movements other than clapping.

• To extend the vocabulary of the game, use pictures instead of actual
objects. To get double duty out of the activity, you may prefer to use
pictures that are tied to a theme being studied in your classroom. For
example, if studying the state of Texas, you might include pictures of
boots, cacti, bluebonnets, and armadillos.

• As your group develops proficiency with this activity, ask one child
both to clap the name of the object and respond with the number of
syllables and ask the others to decide if the first child is correct.

• Using the top row of a pocket chart, arrange number cards to display
the numbers 1, 2, 3, 4, and 5, from left to right. Have a child pull a picture card from the basket and, using the same procedure as for the

objects, clap and count the number of syllables. The child must then place the picture card beneath the correct number card in the pocket chart. Review the pictures, from left to right, once the row has been completed.

- After the children become very comfortable with this activity, let them try to determine the number of syllables in words without clapping or saying the words aloud. This is quite difficult because it removes the kinesthetic aspect, forcing the children instead to "hear" the words in their heads. Notably, many children seem to view this as a problem to be solved and enjoy it as a change when fairly competent with hearing syllables.

NOTES AND ADDITIONAL ACTIVITIES

6C 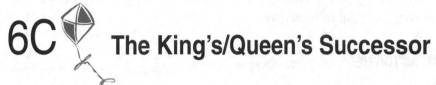 The King's/Queen's Successor

Objective

To bring out the rhythm of the words through repeated movement

Materials needed

Toy or paper crown

Activity

Make a crown for the designated king or queen to wear. At the beginning of the game, ask all of the children to stand in a circle around you. Acting as the king or queen, issue an order (i.e., an action word), cleanly pausing between the syllables. The children are then to do the action in time to the syllables (e.g., *march-ing, march-ing, march-ing*). The words need to be said very rhythmically so that everyone is in time with each other. Once you have shown everyone how to play, ask the children to take turns wearing the crown and issuing the orders. In initial play, we recommend that you use the following words:

boogy-woogying	leaning	sewing
bowing	marching	stretching
clapping	nodding	tiptoeing
curtsying	reading	waddling
hammering	roller-skating	waving
hippity-hopping	rotating	wiggling
hokey-pokeying	saluting	

Variation

• Introduce an action word (e.g., *swaying*), and ask the children to clap and count its syllables. If there are two syllables, as in *sway-ing*, suggest a movement that has two parts (e.g., move to one side, then the other).

After you have demonstrated several words in this way, have the children take turns wearing the crown and thinking of words and actions. The child who is king or queen goes to the middle of the circle, states the action word, claps it, determines the number of syllables, and then demonstrates his or her idea of actions matching the number of syllables.

Note: The focus of this game is on the children's awareness of syllables. Do not be concerned if the movement suggested by the child bears no relation to the word's meaning, so long as it captures the word's syllabic structure.

NOTES AND ADDITIONAL ACTIVITIES

6D Listening First, Looking After

Objective

To show students how to synthesize syllables spoken one by one into familiar words

Materials needed

Pictures of objects familiar to the children

Activity

This game requires a set of pictures, each depicting a familiar object. Choose pictures of objects that have names of differing syllables. Hold up your stack of pictures and explain that you will say the name of each but in a very strange way—one syllable at a time. Encourage the children to listen carefully and to figure out each picture named.

In naming each picture, speak in a strict monotone and insert a clear pause between each syllable (e.g., *tel-e-phone*). When the children figure out each word, hold up the picture and have the children repeat the word in both normal and syllable-by-syllable fashion.

Note: Your students are likely to master this game quickly. If so, play only a couple of times before moving on to other activities.

NOTES AND ADDITIONAL ACTIVITIES

6E 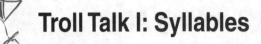 Troll Talk I: Syllables

Objective   To reinforce students' ability to synthesize words from their separate syllables

Activity   Invite everyone to sit in a circle, and engage them in a story:

> Once upon a time there was a kind, little troll who loved to give people presents. The only catch was that the troll always wanted people to know what their present was before giving it to them. The problem was that the little troll had a very strange way of talking. If he was going to tell a child that the present was a bicycle, he would say "*bi-cy-cle.*" Not until the child had guessed what the present was would he be completely happy.

Now, pretend to be the troll and go around the room, presenting a "present" each child, pronouncing the name of the present syllable by syllable. When the child guesses the word, she or he is to name a present for somebody else. It is best to limit the game to only four or five children on any given day, or it becomes a bit long. Examples of gifts to pronounce include the following:

Barbie	coconuts	rhinoceroses
baseball	computer	roller skates
basketball	fingerpaints	spaghetti
bicycle	Frisbee	television
boomerang	guitar	trampoline
broccoli	hippopotamus	ukulele
bubble bath	Nintendo	watermelon
camera	peppermint	xylophone
chocolate	refrigerator	yo-yo

Note: If the students are not familiar with trolls, then substitute another person or creature from folklore such as a leprechaun, unicorn, or elf.

7 Initial and Final Sounds

The activities in this chapter introduce the children to the nature and existence of phonemes. The games are designed, first, to lead the children to discover that words contain phonemes and, second, to help them begin to learn about the phonemes' separate identities so that they can recognize them and distinguish them one from another.

Because the identities and distinguishing characteristics of the phonemes are easier to feel in one's mouth than to hear with one's ears, the children's attention should be directed and redirected to the phonemes' articulation. The children should be repeatedly encouraged to explore, compare, and contrast the phonemes' place and manner of articulation. Over and over, throughout the activities in this chapter, they should be asked, "What are you doing with your lips, tongue, mouth, and voice as you make the sound of /m/, /b/, /p/?" and so forth.

Because the initial phonemes of words are easier to distinguish and attend to than medial or final phonemes, the first few games in this chapter concentrate on them. Further along in the chapter, the same games are repeated with final consonants.

Final consonants are relatively difficult to isolate even when they are meticulously enunciated. Exacerbating this difficulty, however, is that most speakers are sloppy about articulating them in running speech; many tend to omit them entirely as a matter of dialect or habit. These sounds, in other words, warrant special attention in the classroom, for children cannot be expected to discover them on their own.

Although the insights and sensitivities targeted by the games in this chapter represent but a first step in the development of phonemic awareness, it is also a critical step and, for many children, a very difficult step. Therefore, while conducting these games, it is extremely important to give all children the opportunity to think of the response on their own; do not let anybody call out answers until you signal. Similarly, because it is so important to detect any children who are having difficulty with the phonemes, remember to use the strategy of switching unpredictably between group and individual responding. Find time to give extra help and practice to those who need it.

7A   Guess Who

Objective

To introduce two key concepts: 1) how phonemes sound when spoken in isolation, and 2) that phonemes are parts of words

Activity

The objectives of this game are built into its structure. To play, the children must attend closely and discriminatively to the phonemes while trying to connect them to the names of which they are part. With all of the children seated in a circle, say "Guess whose name I'm going to say now." Then secretly choose the name of one of the students and distinctly enunciate its initial phoneme only. For names beginning with a stop consonant, such as Dick, the phoneme should be repeated over and over, clearly and distinctly: "/d/ /d/ /d/ /d/ /d/." Continuant consonants should be stretched as well as repeated (e.g., "/s-s-s-s/ /s-s-s-s/ /s-s-s-s/ /s-s-s-s/"). If more than one child's name has the same initial sound, encourage the children to guess all of the possibilities. This introduces the point that every phoneme shows up in lots of different words.

Variation

- Once the game is familiar, you may pass control to the children. After a given child's name is guessed, she or he may give the hint for the next name: "I'm thinking of someone's name that begins with [sound]."

NOTES AND ADDITIONAL ACTIVITIES

7B   Different Words, Same Initial Phoneme

Objective

To reinforce the concept that each phoneme shows up in many different words and to invite the children to pay attention to how the phonemes feel when they are articulated

Materials needed

Picture cards for each targeted phoneme

Activity

Gather a set of three or four pictures for each phoneme you want the children to explore. For example, you might choose pictures of a fox, a foot, some feathers, and a fish for the /f/ set and pictures of a man, a mouse, a mitten, and a moon for the /m/ set.

For the time being, it is important that the name of each picture used begins with a single consonant, preferably a continuant consonant. None of the pictures should begin with consonant blends such as fr-, pl-, or st- because that would make the game too hard for most children at this point.

To play the game, choose one set of pictures and engage the children in the task of identifying the name of each object depicted. Bear in mind that when a word is unfamiliar, it is very difficult to direct attention to its phonemes. Therefore, when there is any doubt about the familiarity of any of these words, ask the class and/or the individual children in concern to repeat it.

After the names of all of the pictures in a set have been agreed on, you should ask a child to pick a picture from the set and name it (e.g., *fox*). Then repeat the name, drawing out the initial consonant (e.g., *f-f-f-f-ox*). Then, ask all of the children to repeat the name in the same way, *f-f-f-f-ox*, and to notice and describe what they are doing with their mouths as they make the /f-f-f/ sound.

Ask another child to choose a picture from the set and name it. Then repeat the name along with the children, drawing out the initial phoneme and attending to its articulation. Then review the pictures chosen thus far, asking, "Do these two words begin with the same sound? What sound do they begin with? Yes, both start with the sound /f-f-f-f/."

This is an especially useful activity both for introducing or clarifying specific phonemes and for working with children who are having special difficulty in conceiving the phonemes. Even so, it is wise to do only a few sets of pictures in a sitting or the children's attention will begin to wander.

Variation   • Pass out pictures to the children. Each must name her or his picture in the style described above (e.g., *f-f-f-f-ish*). This game works well with small groups.

NOTES AND ADDITIONAL ACTIVITIES

7C  Finding Things: Initial Phonemes

Objective To extend the children's awareness of initial phonemes by asking them to compare, contrast, and eventually identify the initial sounds of a variety of words

Materials needed Picture cards

Activity This game should be played as an extension of Activity 7B: Different Words, Same Initial Phoneme. Spread a few pictures out in the middle of the circle. Then ask the children to find those pictures whose names start with the initial sound on which they have just been working. As each picture is found, the child is to say its name and initial phoneme as before (e.g., *f-f-f-f-ish, /f-f-f-f/, fish*).

Variations
- As the children become more comfortable with the game, spread out pictures from two different sets, asking the children to identify the name and initial phoneme of each picture and to sort them into two piles accordingly.

- Pass pictures out to the children; each must identify the initial phoneme of her or his picture and put it in the corresponding pile. This game works well with small groups.

- Sound-tration: Pass pictures of objects or animals to the children, naming each picture and placing it face down on the table or carpet. Children take turns flipping pairs of pictures right side up and deciding if the initial sounds of the picture's names are the same. If the initial sounds match, the child selects another pair; otherwise, another child takes a turn. This game works well with small groups.

7D 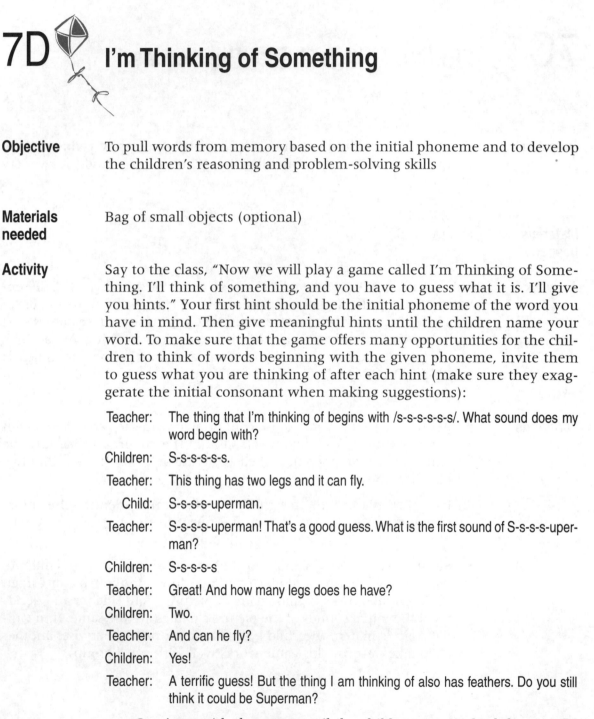 I'm Thinking of Something

Objective To pull words from memory based on the initial phoneme and to develop the children's reasoning and problem-solving skills

Materials needed Bag of small objects (optional)

Activity Say to the class, "Now we will play a game called I'm Thinking of Something. I'll think of something, and you have to guess what it is. I'll give you hints." Your first hint should be the initial phoneme of the word you have in mind. Then give meaningful hints until the children name your word. To make sure that the game offers many opportunities for the children to think of words beginning with the given phoneme, invite them to guess what you are thinking of after each hint (make sure they exaggerate the initial consonant when making suggestions):

Teacher: The thing that I'm thinking of begins with /s-s-s-s-s-s/. What sound does my word begin with?

Children: S-s-s-s-s-s.

Teacher: This thing has two legs and it can fly.

Child: S-s-s-s-uperman.

Teacher: S-s-s-s-uperman! That's a good guess. What is the first sound of S-s-s-s-uperman?

Children: S-s-s-s-s

Teacher: Great! And how many legs does he have?

Children: Two.

Teacher: And can he fly?

Children: Yes!

Teacher: A terrific guess! But the thing I am thinking of also has feathers. Do you still think it could be Superman?

Continue with the game until the children name a bird that can fly and whose name begins with /s-s-s-s/ (e.g., *seagull, s-s-s-seagull*). As the children become better at the game, let them review each suggestion among themselves by asking, "Could that be it? Does that match all the hints?" Do no more than two or three words each time the game is played.

Variation
- Using a sack full of objects, say "Guess what's in my bag. It begins with /d-d-d-d/ and it swims." Children make guesses based on clues as above. At the end of the game, the initial sounds of all objects are reviewed.

NOTES AND ADDITIONAL ACTIVITIES

7E Word Pairs I: Take a Sound Away (Analysis)

Objective To help the children to separate the sounds of words from their meanings

Activity By showing the children that if the initial phoneme of a word is removed a totally different word may result, this activity further helps children to separate the sounds of words from their meanings. With the children seated in a circle, explain that sometimes when you take a sound away from a word, you end up with a totally different word. To give the children an example, say *"f-f-f-f-ear,"* elongating the initial consonant, and have the children repeat. Then say *"ear,"* and have the children repeat. Ask the children if they can determine which sound has been taken away and repeat the words for them (i.e., *f-f-f-f-ear . . . ear . . . f-f-f-f . . . ear . . . ear*).

In this way, the children are challenged to attend to the initial phonemes of words even as they come to realize that the presence or absence of the initial phoneme results in two different words. Across days, gradually work up from the easier initial consonants to harder ones. Sample word lists are provided at the end of the chapter on pages 69–70.

Note: Most children can identify the "hidden word" but have a great deal of difficulty in identifying what is taken away. Children may also be inclined to produce rhyming words rather than to focus on initial sounds. With this in mind, take care not to flip back and forth between the activities involving rhyming and initial sounds.

Variations

- To help the children notice that the initial sound makes a big difference in the words' meanings, ask them to use each word in a sentence.

- When the children are comfortable with this game, play it with game 7I: Spider's Web.

- Call the children to line up by naming their first names without the initial sound (e.g., *[J]-onathon*). The children have to figure out whose name has been called and what sound is missing. You may want to delete initial blends as a unit until after blends have been introduced in Chapter 8 (e.g., *[St]-anley*).

7F Word Pairs II: Add a Sound (Synthesis)

Objective   To introduce the children to the challenge of synthesizing words from their separate phonemes

Activity   Seat the children in a circle, and begin by explaining that sometimes a new word can be made by adding a sound to a word. As an example, say "*ox*," and have the children repeat it. Then ask what will happen if they add a new sound to the beginning of the word such as /f-f-f-f-f/: "*f-f-f-f-f . . . ox, f-f-f-f . . . ox, f-f-f-f-ox.*" The children say "*fox!*" You should then explain, "We put a new sound on the beginning, and we have a new word!"

Until the children catch on, you should provide solid guidance, asking the children to say the word parts with you in unison (e.g., "*ice . . . m-m-m-m . . . ice . . . m-m-m-ice . . . mice*"). Again, it is appropriate to work up gradually, across days, from the easier initial consonants to harder ones and, only after the latter are reasonably well established, to consonant blends (e.g., *mile–smile*).

Variations   • Invite the children to use each word of a pair in a sentence to emphasize the difference in their meanings.

• When the children are good at this, play it with 7I: Spider's Web.

NOTES AND ADDITIONAL ACTIVITIES

Initial/Final Sounds

65

7G Different Words, Same Final Phoneme

Objective To lead the children to discover the identities of word-final phonemes by exploring their articulation

Materials needed Picture cards

Activity The game is played just like game 7B: Different Words, Same Initial Phoneme, except that the object is to identify words that end in the same phoneme. To play the game, you will need to gather sets of three or four pictures that depict objects that end with the same phoneme. For example, the /m/ set might include pictures of a ham, a comb, a lamb, and a broom.

Note: Final phonemes are much more difficult to hear or feel than initial phonemes. For this reason, work with the final phonemes should be deferred until the children are comfortable with initial phoneme activities. Do not, however, be tempted to neglect these games because awareness of final phonemes is an important entry to the level of phonemic awareness that supports able decoding and spelling.

NOTES AND ADDITIONAL ACTIVITIES

7H 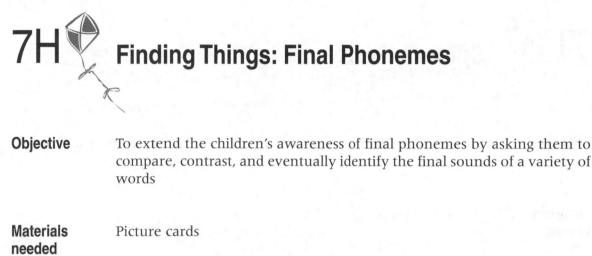 Finding Things: Final Phonemes

Objective

To extend the children's awareness of final phonemes by asking them to compare, contrast, and eventually identify the final sounds of a variety of words

Materials needed

Picture cards

Activity

This game should be played just like game 7C: Finding Things: Initial Phonemes, except that the focus is on the final phonemes. Spread a few pictures out in the middle of the circle. Then ask the children to find those pictures whose names end with a specified final phoneme. As each picture is found, the child should say its name and final phoneme (e.g., *"rain-n-n-n . . . n-n-n-n . . . rain-n-n"*).

Variations

- Play this game with the additional hints of the initial sounds and/or the number of syllables. For example, "I'm thinking of something that begins with /s-s-s-s/ and has two syllables and ends with /d d d d/.

- As the children become more comfortable with the game, spread out pictures from two different sets, asking the children to identify the name and final phoneme of each picture and to sort them into two piles accordingly.

- Pass pictures out to the children, and ask each to identify the final phoneme of her or his picture and put it in the corresponding pile. This game works well with small groups.

7l Spider's Web

Objective To detect any children who are still struggling with the phonemes and to offer some physical amusement for the children

Materials needed Ball of yarn or string

Activity This game adds challenge and interest to the two word pair games (7E: Word Pairs I: Take a Sound Away [Analysis], and 7F: Word Pairs II: Add a Sound [Synthesis]). Have the children sit in a circle and roll a ball of yarn from one to another as each responds. Gradually, as the ball of yarn is rolled from child to child, a large spider's web is created within the circle of children. When a complete web has been made, it can be lifted up high, and you can engage the children in a song about a spider. Finally, the ball of yarn is rolled up again from child to child.

If the whole class is part of the web, the web can be impressive, but it does take a long time. Spider's Web may be more manageable in small groups because less time is spent rerolling yarn and distances are shorter—both important considerations with young children.

Note: The children should be fairly successful with at least the beginning levels of the previous two games. In addition, it is a good idea to let them practice with the spider's web several times before doing this game.

With Word Pair I Remind the children that sometimes a new word can be created by taking away the first sound of some other word. Then go through a couple of examples with the children from 7E: Word Pairs I: Take a Sound Away (Analysis). After this review, the game can start.

Say a word pair (e.g., "r-r-r-ice/ice"). Have all the children repeat it. Holding on to the loose end, roll a ball of yarn to one child and ask, "What sound did I take away?" The child should catch the yarn and say *"r-r-r-ice . . . ice . . . r-r-r."* If the child is unsure, you should repeat and assist as necessary. Then say a new word that the children repeat, and the child who has the yarn ball rolls it to another child while holding onto the yarn.

With Word Pair II

Remind the children that sometimes a new word can be created by adding a sound to the beginning of some other word. Then go through a couple of examples with the children from 7F: Word Pairs II: Add a Sound (Synthesis). After this review, the game can start.

Say, "*m-m-m . . . old.*" Have the children repeat this. Then roll the ball to a child who is to respond "*m . . . old, mold.*" Continuing the game, say, for example, "*f-f-f . . . arm.*" All of the children repeat what you have said, and the child with the yarn rolls it on to another child who catches it and says "*f-f-f . . . arm/farm.*" The following are examples of word pairs beginning with easy consonant onsets:

chin–in	mask–ask	Sam–am
fair–air	mat–at	same–aim
farm–arm	Max–ax	sand–and
fat–at	meal–eel	seal–eel
feel–eel	meat–eat	seat–eat
fold–old	mice–ice	shake–ache
fox–ox	mill–ill	share–air
hair–air	moan–own	sheet–eat
hand–and	more–oar	shin–in
hate–ate	name–aim	shout–out
heart–art	near–ear	show–oh
hoops–oops	neat–eat	shy–eye
kneel–eel	nice–ice	sink–ink
knit–it	nod–odd	thick–ick
land–and	now–ow	think–ink
lend–end	phone–own	vase–ace
make–ache	race–ace	woight–eight
mash–ash	rice–ice	wheel–eel

The following are examples of word pairs beginning with harder consonant onsets:

beat–eat	case–ace	pit–it
bend–end	cold–old	pitch–itch
band–and	cow–ow	poke–oak
boil–oil	game–aim	take–ache
bone–own	lake–ache	tall–all
bus–us	part–art	told–old
care–air	pat–at	towel–owl

Then explain to the children that sometimes a new word can be created by adding a sound to the end of some other word. Say "*bark-k-k-k . . . k-k-k . . . barkkk.*" Have the children repeat this. Then roll the ball of yarn to a child who is to respond "*bar . . . k, bark.*" Continue the game by saying, for example, "*tooth-th-th . . . th-th-th . . . toothththth.*" All of the children repeat what you have said, and the child with the yarn rolls it to another child who catches it and says *"too . . . th, tooth."* The following are examples of word pairs for final consonant games:

bar–bark	gray–grape	no–note
bay–bake	gray–great	say–safe
bee–beak	her–hurt	say–same
bee–bean	hoe–hope	say–save
bee–beef	hoe–hose	see–seal
boo–boot	how–house	see–seed
buy–bike	lay–lace	see–seek
buy–bite	lay–lake	she–sheet
car–card	lay–late	she–sheep
car–cart	me–meal	sigh–side
coal–cold	me–mean	sigh–sight
die–dime	me–meat	so–soap
far–farm	moo–mood	tie–tight
four–fork	moo–moon	tie–time
free–freeze	moo–moose	tray–trace
go–goat	my–mice	tree–treat
goo–goose	my–might	two–toot
gray–grain	no–nose	two–tooth

NOTES AND ADDITIONAL ACTIVITIES

8 Phonemes

Understanding how the alphabetic principle works depends on understanding that all words are composed of strings of phonemes. In terms of raw logic, this is not very different from understanding that sentences are composed of strings of words and words of strings of syllables. Phonemes, however, are much more difficult for children to perceive or conceptualize than words or syllables.

Phonemes are the smallest functional units of speech, which may be one of the reasons that they are so hard to notice. But there are other reasons as well. First, unlike words, phonemes are meaningless; therefore, it is unnatural to lend them active attention in the course of typical speaking or listening. Second, unlike syllables, phonemes cannot be easily distinguished in running speech; therefore, it is difficult for children to understand what to listen for even when trying. Worse, phonemes are so acoustically variable that every one of them sounds more or less different from one speaker to the next and from one word to the next.

Again, phonemes are best distinguished less by how they sound than by how they are articulated. For this reason, children should be encouraged to explore how their voices and the positions of their mouths and tongues change with each sound. Invite the children to look at each other while saying a given phoneme, or give them hand mirrors to examine the movement of their own mouths. The more approaches that are used, the greater the likelihood that each child will find his or her own way to understand the nature of the phonemes.

For most of the activities in this chapter, it is additionally recommended that the children use blocks to represent the separate phonemes. The blocks can also be replaced with bingo disks, cardboard squares, or whatever else is handy. Their purpose is only to give the children some concrete, tangible representation for sorting the phonemes one from another.

The first several games use words with only two sounds, allowing the children to experiment with the phonemes both in isolation and as blended in minimal phonological contexts. In the second set of activities, consonants are added to the two-sound words to make simple, closed syllables such as *mice* and *cat*. You are likely to notice a tendency for the children to lose the vowel phonemes in analyzing these words. Although this tendency is normal at this stage, you should take care to correct it. As they move into independent spelling, children should remember that every syllable needs a vowel. The children's attention is next directed to the structure of consonant blends. Because the notion that consonant blends are made up of sequences of separate phonemes is generally quite difficult for young children, it is the focus of two separate sets of activities. Finally, having established these basics, the remaining activities are designed to refine and strengthen the children's cognitive flexibility in phoneme analysis and synthesis.

These games are intended to develop a level of phonemic awareness that is of well-documented and significant benefit to young readers and writers. Be warned, however, that the attendant challenges are also extremely difficult for some children. Monitor the performance and progress of each of your students carefully and continuously as you play each game. Children who are experiencing difficulty should immediately receive extra attention and support. Across the chapter, a number of variations are suggested, including ways that more advanced students can play among themselves. Take advantage of these games to create opportunities to work more intensively with the others, whether individually or in small groups.

8A   Two-Sound Words

Objective

To introduce the children to the challenges of analyzing syllables into phonemes and of synthesizing syllables from phonemes

Materials needed

Blocks
Two-phoneme word cards

Activity

The two-sound games serve to introduce the procedure and logic of the more difficult phonemic analysis and synthesis activities that follow. In addition, two-sound words provide an unfettered medium for giving children practice with the sounds of the various phonemes, both in isolation and as blended together in phonologically minimal words. In view of this, it is more helpful to revisit them as needed by individuals or by the group than to dwell too long in any given session. Because of their foundational importance, however, it is critical that every child grasp this concept before moving on to the more advanced activities.

On the first day, it is sufficient to do analysis only. On subsequent days, begin with analysis and shift to synthesis. Similarly, for the first few days, it is wise to separate play with initial consonant words from play with final consonant words for clarity. Once the children have caught on, the two types of words should be freely intermixed. Finally, because the short vowels are so much more variable and less distinctive in both sound and articulation, their introduction should be deferred until the children are reasonably comfortable with long-vowel words. Again, to clarify the children's image of the phonemes and to support their ability to distinguish them one from another, it is valuable to ask them to feel how their mouths change position with each sound or to look at their mouths in a mirror while saying the words. In addition, as in all of the phonemic awareness activities, it is important to ensure that the students are familiar with each word used in these exercises. If you suspect that any of your students are not, it is wise to review the word's meaning and usage.

Phonemes

Note: To play these games, each of the children should have two blocks. In addition, you should have two blocks of your own and a set of pictures of two-phoneme words. Also, before beginning, it is important to have read the introduction to this chapter.

Analysis

A child picks a card and names what it depicts. For this example, let us assume that the child chooses a picture of a hair bow. You would repeat the word, but slowly and with a clear pause (about a half-second interval) between its two phonemes (e.g., "*b . . . ō*"). Then all of the children should repeat the word in this same manner, "*b . . . ō . . .*" To show that the word *bow* consists of two separate sounds, the teacher now places blocks in two different colors underneath the picture as she enunciates the sound represented by each.

The children then repeat the word sound by sound while representing the sounds of the word, left to right, with their own blocks. The children should repeat the sounds while pointing to the respective blocks and then the word, pausing slightly less between phonemes with each repetition (e.g., "*b . . . . ō . . . , bow, b . . . ō . . bow, b . . ō, bow, b-ō . . . bow*").

Synthesis

This game is just the reverse of the analysis game and likewise requires that you model the procedure before turning it over to the children. Choose a picture and place it face down so the children cannot see it. Then name the picture, phoneme by phoneme (e.g., "*b . . . ō*"), while placing the blocks beneath the picture. While pointing to their own blocks, the children must repeat the phonemes over and over and faster and faster as they did in the analysis game. When they believe they know the identity of the picture, they should raise their hands. The teacher may then ask the group or any individual to name the picture. After resolving any disagreements, the picture is held up for all to see.

After modeling several words in this way, pass the challenge to the children. For each new picture, help them agree on its name and give them time to analyze it on their own. To gain a good sense of who is and is not catching on, ask one or more individuals to share his or her solution to each word. Then the whole group should repeat the solution together, voicing the separate phonemes of the word as they point to their corresponding blocks.

Variations

- Extend the exercises to unpictured words. At the outset of each analysis challenge, be sure to use each in a sentence for the sake of clarity (e.g., "Chew. Please *chew* your food before you swallow it. Chew."). Similarly, ask the children to use each word in a sentence as part of the wrap-up of each synthesis challenge.

- Later, this game can be used to teach the alphabetic principle by replacing the colored blocks with letter tokens. If you choose to do so, however, bear in mind that to convey the essential logic of the alphabetic principle, it is best that all words include one letter for each sound, left to right. With this in mind, avoid words with silent letters or digraphs. Use only short vowel words and, among those, only those that are spelled with two letters (e.g., *in* and *am* are fine, but not *edge* or *itch*).

Note: All of the words in the following lists consist of only two phonemes. Nevertheless, due to the vagaries of English, the spellings of many involve more than two letters. For this reason, showing the words' spellings will only confuse the issue for now. The following are examples of two-sound words with initial consonants and long vowels:

day	bee	bye	bow	show
hay	fee	die	doe	toe
jay	gee	guy	go	boo
may	he	hi	hoe	chew
pay	knee	lie	low	coo
ray	me	my	mow	do
say	pea	pie	no	goo
way	see	rye	row	moo
	she	sigh	/r⁻o/	shoe
	tea	tie	sew	two
	we	why	/s⁻o/	who

The following are examples of two-sound words with final consonants and long vowels:

ace	each
ache	ease
age	eat
aid	eel
ail	ice
aim	oak
ape	oat
eight	own

The following are examples of two-sound words with final consonants and short vowels:

add	Ed	itch
am	ick	odd
an	if	off
as	ill	on
ash	in	up
at	is	us
edge	it	

8B Basic Three-Sound Words

Objective

To extend phoneme analysis and synthesis to consonant-vowel-consonant words

Activity

To play this game, you and each of the children will need three blocks. Start by saying a two-sound word (e.g., *ice*) in two clearly separate parts, "*ī . . . s*," asking the children to repeat what you have said. All the children should then represent the word with two blocks of different colors to show that it consists of two sounds.

Next explain that words may consist of more than two sounds. To demonstrate, say the word *rice*, "*r . . . ī . . . s*," and ask the children to repeat the word in unison. To represent the third phoneme, place a new block to the left of the two other blocks, pronouncing the whole word, phoneme by phoneme, as you point to each block in turn from left to right (reading direction).

Following this introduction, the activity is divided into three different stages. In the first stage, analysis to synthesis, children are led to notice that a new word can be created by adding another phoneme to a two-sound word. The second stage, synthesis to analysis, demonstrates that one can, conversely, make a two-sound word by removing one consonant from a three-sound word. The third stage of the activity, analysis and synthesis, requires the children to use this knowledge to determine the number of sounds in two- and three-phoneme words on their own.

Analysis to Synthesis

Pronounce a two-phoneme word and use it in a sentence to ensure its recognition (e.g., "Eat. I *eat* lunch"). The children should repeat the word and, working with their colored blocks, analyze it into its separate phonemes. Review the children's solutions with them, making sure that all have divided the word properly and know how to recite it with the blocks, left to right: "*ē . . . t*."

Phoneme by phoneme, next produce a new word, created by adding a consonant to the first (e.g., "*s . . . ē . . . t*"). The children's challenge is to modify their block arrangement to represent this new, three-sound word. While pointing to their respective blocks, the children then repeat the three phonemes over and over and faster and faster in sequence, just as they learned to do in the two-sound games. When they have succeeded in blending the phonemes together and recognizing your word, they should raise their hands, prepared to name it and to use it in a sentence. You must take care to call on different children for each word, providing help and encouragement to each as needed.

Synthesis to Analysis

Slowly, distinctly, and phoneme by phoneme, pronounce a three-phoneme word (e.g., "*n . . . ā . . . m*"). The children represent the three phonemes with their blocks, and repeat them in sequence until they synthesize the word *name*. As soon as the word is recognized, the children should raise their hands, prepared to name it and use it in a sentence.

Then pronounce a two-phoneme word, created by removing one of the consonants (e.g., *aim*). After the children have modified their block arrangements to represent the new word, they should raise their hands, prepared to share their solution, phoneme by phoneme: "*ā . . . m.*" Again, take care to call on one or more different children for each word, providing help and encouragement to each as needed.

Analysis and Synthesis

Select a rhyming pair, including one two- and one three-phoneme word, such as *each* and *teach*. Choose one of the words—sometimes the longer and sometimes the shorter—and present it to the children for analysis (e.g., "Teach. I *teach* fabulously"). After the children have analyzed the word and represented its phonemes with their blocks, ask the group (or an individual) to review the solution by pointing to each block while sounding its corresponding phoneme. When all have corrected their arrangements, present the other member of the rhyming pair (e.g., "*ē . . . ch*"). The children must modify their block arrangements appropriately and then use them to synthesize your second word. When they have figured it out, they should raise their hands, prepared to name it and use it in a sentence.

Note: It is important that the children not be able to guess whether the shorter or longer word will be presented first. A primary value of this game is in challenging them to determine the number of phonemes in each word on their own.

Variations

- Place two pictures on the table. The children must decide which of the pictures represents the word with the most sounds by placing their own blocks in front of them while sounding the words aloud. As necessary, you may help them by sounding the words at the same time while placing a block for each sound beneath the respective pictures. Make sure the children arrange and "read" their own blocks in the reading direction from left to right.

Phonemes

Once familiar, this variation can be given to small groups of children to play among themselves, affording you the opportunity to give special attention to others who need it.

- Challenge the children to decide whether unpictured words consist of two or three phonemes by presenting pairs such as *ice–mice, eat–meat,* and *so–soap.* Take care to vary whether the longer or shorter word of each pair is presented first. After deciding the answer, the children should corroborate their responses by explicitly analyzing the words. If supported by pairs of picture cards, this variation can also be given to small groups of children to play with among themselves.

- Lay out 10 pictures of a suitable degree of difficulty in the middle of the table. Have the children take turns "thinking" of one of the words and sounding it out (with blocks). The other children are to figure out which picture was in mind. The child who names the picture gets to keep it as a "prize."

- Later, the basic three-sound activities can be used to teach the alphabetic principle by replacing the colored blocks with letter tokens. If you choose to do so, use only short vowel words and, even among those, avoid any that involve digraphs or silent letters. Again, it is best that all words include one letter for each sound, left to right. Following are examples of words for adding initial consonants:

ice	**am**	**an**	**in**
mice	ham	ban	chin
nice	jam	Dan	shin
rice	Sam	fan	win
		man	
eat	**ate**	pan	**eel**
heat	bait	ran	deal
meat	gate	tan	feel
seat	hate	van	heel
wheat	late		meal
	wait	**ad**	real
up		fad	seal
cup	**own**	lad	wheel
pup	bone	mad	
	cone	pad	**ill**
it	moan	sad	Bill
bit	phone	Tad	chill
fit			fill
hit	**ash**	**itch**	pill
kit	dash	ditch	will
pit	gnash	pitch	
sit	mash	rich	**edge**
wit	rash	witch	hedge

The following are examples of words for adding final consonants:

bee	**say**	**tea**	**row**
beach	safe	teach	road
bead	sail	team	roar
bean	same	tease	robe
beef	**moo**	teen	rose
beet	mood	teeth	**so**
May	moon	**ray**	soak
made	moose	rail	soap
mail	**way**	rain	soar
make	wade	rake	**he**
mane	wail	**two**	heap
knee	wait	tool	hear
near	wake	toot	heat
neat	**lie**	tooth	heel
need	life	**toe**	**my**
no	light	toad	mice
nose	like	toes	might
note	lime	tore	mine

NOTES AND ADDITIONAL ACTIVITIES

8C Consonant Blends: Adding and Subtracting Initial Sounds

Objective   To introduce the children to the phonemic structure of consonant blends

Activity   Again, give yourself and each child three blocks. The activity is divided into three different stages and is played much like 8B: Basic Three-Sound Words. In the first stage, children are led to notice that consonant blends can be created by adding one consonant before another. The second stage demonstrates that they can, conversely, remove the first consonant from a blend. The third stage of the activity requires the children to use this knowledge to determine the number of sounds in words that do or do not begin with consonant blends.

Analysis to Synthesis   Pronounce a two-phoneme word that begins with a consonant and use it in a sentence to ensure its recognition (e.g., "Lay: I *lay* down on my bed"). Have the children repeat the word and, working with their blocks, analyze it into its separate phonemes. Then invite the children to review their analyses, making sure that all have divided the word properly: "*l . . . ā.*"

Phoneme by phoneme, produce a new word that rhymes with the first but begins with a consonant blend. The new word should be presented phoneme by phoneme (e.g., "*p . . . l . . . ā*"). The children's challenge is to modify their block arrangement to represent this new, three-sound word. While pointing to their respective blocks, the children then repeat the three phonemes over and over and faster and faster in sequence, just as they learned to do in the previous games. When they have succeeded in blending the phonemes together and recognizing your word, they should raise their hands and prepare themselves to use the word in a sentence.

Because of the special difficulty of understanding the nature of consonant blends, the members of each pair should be explicitly reviewed and compared before moving on. This should be done by repeatedly removing and replacing the leftmost block as the two words are enunciated in time: "*lay . . . play . . . lay . . . play . . . lay . . . play.*"

Synthesis to Analysis   Slowly, distinctly, and phoneme by phoneme, pronounce a three-phoneme word that begins with a consonant blend (e.g., "g . . . r . . . ō"). The children should represent the three phonemes with their blocks and repeat them in sequence until they synthesize the word *grow*. Then produce a two-phoneme rhyme by removing one of the consonants (e.g., "*row*"). After the children have modified their block arrangements to represent the new word, they should raise their hands, prepared to share their solution, phoneme by phoneme: "r . . . ō." Again, take care to call on different children to present the solution to each word, providing help and encouragement to each as needed.

Analysis and Synthesis   Select a rhyming pair, including one two- and one three-phoneme word, such as *no* and *snow*. Choose one of the words—sometimes the longer and sometimes the shorter—and present it to the children for analysis (e.g., "*No. No, no,* I won't go"). After the children have analyzed the word and represented its phonemes with their blocks, ask the group (or an individual) to review the solution by pointing to each block while sounding its corresponding phoneme. When all have corrected their arrangements, present the other member of the rhyming pair (e.g., "s . . . n . . . ō"). The children must modify their block arrangements appropriately and then use them to synthesize the second word. When they have figured it out, they should raise their hands, prepared to name it and use it in a sentence.

Note: It is important that the children not be able to guess whether the shorter or longer word will be presented first. A primary value of this game is in challenging them to determine the number of phonemes in each word on their own.

Variations
- As the children gain proficiency, intermix words from 8B: Basic Three-Sound Words: Analysis and Synthesis (Stage 3) and the following variations.

- Adapt the variations described at the end of 8B: Basic Three-Sound Words to these words. Encourage children who are ready, to work in small groups; doing so affords each of them more and more challenging playtime as it affords the teacher an opportunity to give extra help to others who need it.

The following are examples of words to which initial consonants can be added:

no	two	row
snow	stew	crow
		grow
rye	**pie**	
cry	spy	**lay**
dry		clay
fry	**low**	play
try	blow	
	glow	**lie**
ray		fly
gray	**way**	sly
pray	sway	
tray		

NOTES AND ADDITIONAL ACTIVITIES

8D

Consonant Blends: Inserting and Removing Internal Sounds

Objective

To develop explicit awareness of the structure of initial consonant blends by teaching children to insert and remove the internal phonemes

Activity

This activity is to be played in three stages, exactly like the previous game. The only difference, in fact, between this game and the previous (8C: Consonant Blends: Adding and Subtracting Initial Sounds) is that the two- and three-sound words in this activity differ in an internal rather than an initial sound (e.g., *so* versus *slow*). Hearing the internal consonant of a blend is far more difficult than hearing the initial consonant. In addition, inserting or removing the internal consonant of a blend requires a new level of phonemic awareness, involving explicit reflective appreciation of the structure of consonant blends. It is in recognition of the special attention that it warrants that we have chosen to treat this challenge as a separate activity.

Again, begin by giving yourself and each of the children three colored blocks. In the first stage, children are led to notice that consonant blends can be created by a second phoneme *after* the first (e.g., *so* versus *slow*). The second stage demonstrates that one can, conversely, *remove* the second phoneme from a blend (e.g., *slow* versus *so*). The third stage of the activity requires the children to use this knowledge to determine the number of sounds in words that do or do not begin with consonant blends. Recognizing the special difficulty of analyzing the consonant blends as required in the third stage, you should monitor the children's performance with extra care and support.

Analysis to Synthesis

Pronounce a two-phoneme word that begins with a consonant and use it in a sentence to ensure its recognition (e.g., "Say. I *say* hello"). Encourage the children to repeat the word and, using the colored blocks, analyze it into its separate phonemes. Then invite the children to review their analyses, making sure that all have divided the word properly: "*s . . . ā*."

Phoneme by phoneme, produce a new word that rhymes with the first but begins with a consonant blend. The new word should be presented phoneme by phoneme (e.g., "*s . . . t . . . ā*"). The children's challenge is to modify their block arrangement to represent this new, three-sound word. While pointing to their respective blocks, the children should then repeat the three phonemes over and over and faster and faster in sequence, just as they learned to do in the previous games. When they have succeeded in blending the phonemes together and recognizing the word, they should raise their hands and prepare themselves to use the word in a sentence.

Because of the special difficulty of understanding the nature of consonant blends, the members of each pair should be explicitly reviewed and compared before moving on. This should be done by repeatedly removing and replacing the leftmost block as the two words are enunciated in time: "say . . . **st**ay . . . say . . . **st**ay . . . say . . . **st**ay."

Synthesis to Analysis

Slowly, distinctly, and phoneme by phoneme, pronounce a three-phoneme word that begins with a consonant blend (e.g., "*g . . . r . . . ō*"). The children represent the three phonemes with their blocks and repeat them in sequence until they synthesize the word *grow*. Then produce a two-phoneme rhyme, created by removing one of the consonants (e.g., *go*). After the children have modified their block arrangements to represent the new word, they should raise their hands, prepared to share their solution, phoneme by phoneme: "*g . . . ō*." Again, take care to call on different children to present the solution to each word, providing help and encouragement to each as needed.

Analysis and Synthesis

Select a rhyming pair, including one two- and one three-phoneme word, such as *go* and *grow*. Choose one of the words—sometimes the longer and sometimes the shorter—and present it to the children for analysis (e.g., "Go. I *go* to school"). After the children have analyzed the word and represented its phonemes with their blocks, ask the group (or an individual) to review the solution by pointing to each block while sounding its corresponding phoneme. When all have corrected their arrangements, present the other member of the rhyming pair (e.g., "*g . . . r . . . ō*"). The children must modify their block arrangements appropriately and then use them to synthesize your second word. When they have figured it out, they should raise their hands, prepared to name it and use it in a sentence.

Note: It is important that the children not be able to guess whether the shorter or longer word will be presented first. A primary value of this game is in challenging them to determine the number of phonemes in each word on their own.

Variations
- As the children gain proficiency, intermix words from 8B: Basic Three-Sound Words, and 8C: Consonant Blends: Adding and Subtracting Initial Sounds, in playing Analysis and Synthesis (Stage 3) and the variations below.

- Adapt the variations described at the end of 8B: Basic Three-Sound Words, to these words. Encourage children who are ready, to work in small groups; doing so affords each of them more and more challenging playtime as it affords the teacher an opportunity to give extra help to others who need it.

Following are examples of words for adding second consonants:

so	**die**	**gay**
slow	dry	gray
snow		**boo**
stow	**tie**	blue
say	try	brew
stay	**see**	**coo**
sway	ski	clue
sigh		crew
sky	**pay**	**two**
sly	play	true
spy	pray	**fee**
sty	**go**	flea
bow	glow	free
blow	grow	

NOTES AND ADDITIONAL ACTIVITIES

Phonemes

8E Building Four-Sound Words

Objective   To extend analysis and synthesis to four-sound words

Activity   To play this game, provide yourself and each of the children with four blocks. Start by saying a three-sound word (e.g., "*spy*") in three clearly separate parts (e.g., "*s . . . p . . . ī*"), asking the children to repeat what you have said. All children should then represent the word with three blocks to show that it consists of three sounds.

Remind the children that, sometimes, a new word can be made by taking a sound away from a three-sound word. As an example, present "*pie*." Ask the children to modify their blocks to represent *pie*. After reviewing the solution, the children are asked to represent *spy* again.

Now explain that, often, new words can also be made by adding a fourth sound to three-sound words. To demonstrate, present the word *spice*, first spoken normally and then phoneme by phoneme: "*Spice. s . . . p . . . ī . . . s.*" To represent the fourth phoneme, place a new block to the right of the other three blocks. Then pronounce each phoneme as you point to each block in turn from left to right (reading direction) and repeat the whole word once more.

Following this introduction, explain that each puzzle in this game starts with a three-sound word. After the children have successfully represented the three-sound word with their blocks, present another word. The new word will be made by either adding a sound or taking a sound away from the three-sound word. They must decide which and figure out what to do to their blocks to represent this new word.

In playing the game, it is important that the children receive feedback on their representations of both the three-sound word and the two- or four-sound word that follows. As usual, this may be done by calling on a student to sound each phoneme of the word while pointing to the block with which it is represented.

The following list provides a number of three-sound words together with two- and four-sound words that can be made from them by taking away or adding a sound. After presenting the three-sound word, follow with either a two- or four-sound word in a way that does not allow the children to predict which it will be. Again, the power of this game is in its implicit requirement that the children listen closely to the phonemes to discover for themselves how many they have heard.

Three-sound words	Two-sound words	Four-sound words
spy	pie	spice
mile	my	smile
peak	pea	speak
gray	ray	great
rain	ray	train
fake	ache	flake
rice	ice	price
pain	pay	paint
grow	row	groan
sly	lie	slime
tray	ray	trace
tone	toe	stone
lace	lay	place
tear	ear	steer
nail	ail	snail
play	pay	plane
seal	eel	steal
inch	in	pinch
late	ate	plate
pill	ill	spill
four	or	fork
art	are	part
are	car	cart
fat	at	flat
stay	say	steak
stew	two	stool
and	an	sand
lake	ache	flake

Variation

- Lay out a number of pictures, each representing a word with a different number of sounds from the others. Choose a child to be "it" (or be "it" yourself). This person should choose a picture, not telling anyone which one, and in his or her mind decide how many sounds it has. Then he or she will say, for example, "I'm thinking of a picture with three sounds." Other children must guess which picture the child is thinking. Again, this is a game that, once familiar, works well with small groups of advanced students.

8F  Guess a Word

Objective

To evaluate the children's progress and confidence in phonemic analysis and segmentation

Activity

Put pictures with one-syllable names face down in the center of a circle with the children seated all around. One child chooses one of the "secret" pictures, not letting others see it. The child then sounds the first phoneme, and everyone repeats. Then she or he sounds the second phoneme, and all repeat. Then the third phoneme (and fourth, for more advanced play) is sounded. After the last phoneme, the group or a chosen individual sounds all of the phonemes in sequence and identifies the secret picture.

Later the pictures can be omitted, and, instead, the teacher can whisper a word to a child who then has to sound the word, phoneme by phoneme, while the other children repeat the phonemes and identify the word.

NOTES AND ADDITIONAL ACTIVITIES

8G Troll Talk II: Phonemes

Objective

To reinforce students' ability to synthesize words from their separate phonemes

Activity

This activity is analogous to that presented in 6E: Troll Talk I: Syllables, except that the troll describes his treats phoneme by phoneme instead of syllable by syllable. Everyone sits in a circle, and the teacher tells a tale:

> Once upon a time, there was a kind, little troll who loved to give people presents. The only catch was that the troll always wanted people to know what their present was before giving it to them. The problem was that the little troll had a very strange way of talking. If he was going to tell a child that the present was a *bike,* he would say "*b . . . ī . . . k.*" Not until the child has guessed what the present was would he be completely happy. Now I will pretend to be the troll. I will name a surprise for one of you. When you figure out what it is, it will be your turn.

Choose one child and pronounce the name of a present, syllable by syllable. When the child guesses the word, she or he is to name a present for somebody else. Work up from short (two- and three-sound) words to longer ones as children become more adept at hearing the sounds. It is best to limit the game to only four or five children on any given day or it becomes a bit long. Examples of gifts include the following:

ape	cheese	moose	soap
bean	desk	pan	stool
book	dog	pea	stump
bow	dress	pen	tie
bread	eel	phone	train
brick	glass	shoe	truck
broom	ice	skate	

Note: If the students are not familiar with trolls, then substitute another person or creature from folklore such as a leprechaun, unicorn, or elf.

Variation   • Each child gets from one to three "secret" pictures. They may now give the things in the pictures as "presents," one thing at a time, to another child by sounding out the word. The child who receives the present has to guess what it is before she or he can have the picture.

NOTES AND ADDITIONAL ACTIVITIES

9 Introducing Letters and Spellings

Because the ultimate purpose of this book is to foster children's reading and writing development, some may find it disconcerting that all of the activities described thus far are focused exclusively on the structure of spoken language. Indeed, some of our readers—especially those who read this book without trying out the activities with their students—may understandably feel a bit impatient at this point. Some may even believe that this approach seems downright inefficient compared with the good old-fashioned tack of teaching children letter-sound correspondences.

Yet, given conventional phonics instruction (i.e., letter-sound correspondences), too many children have great difficulty in learning to blend sounds and to spell. They get stuck and don't understand. Moreover, this happens even among children who have duly learned their letters and their letter-sound correspondences. In fact, it is of little use to memorize the sounds that go with the letters unless one has first gained the insight that every word is made up of a sequence of such sounds. Similarly, it does little good to memorize that the letter *b* sounds like /b/ unless that /b/ is recognized as the sound that is heard in such words as *bubble, ball,* and *banana.*

The purpose of developing children's phonemic awareness is to give children these linguistic insights on which a productive understanding of the alphabetic principle depends. As reviewed previously, research amply documents that this sort of training results in significantly more efficient reading and writing growth for the group as well as a significantly reduced incidence of reading failure.

The design and sequence of the activities in this book are intended to help children acquire a sense of the architecture of their language and the nature of its building blocks. Thus, across chapters, the children's attention is focused and refocused on smaller and smaller parts, on layers within layers of the language. Gradually, they are led to notice how stories are built from sentences, sentences from words, words from syllables, and syllables themselves from a relatively small set of basic speech elements—phonemes. The children are led to see how, within each layer, the parts can be broken apart, separately spoken, and put back together. They are led to see that if the parts are omitted, substituted, or rearranged, then the whole is altered in sound *and* meaning. They are, in short, led to appreciate the structure of the system.

But that's not all. Over the course of all this structural play, the children also learn how to focus on the parts themselves; this is particularly important at the level of the phonemes. As the children practice synthesizing words from phonemes and analyzing phonemes from words, they are also practicing hearing and saying the phonemes over and over, both in isolation and in context. They are becoming generally familiar with how the different phonemes sound and how they are articulated. They are becoming comfortable with hearing and feeling the identity and distinguishing characteristics of each phoneme, whether spoken in isolation or in the beginning, middle, or end of a variety of words.

Research shows that once children have mastered phonemic awareness in this way, useful knowledge of the alphabetic principle generally follows with remarkable ease—and no wonder: Having learned to attend to and think about the structure of language in this way, the alphabetic principle makes sense. All that's left to make it usable is knowledge of the particular letters by which each sound is represented. This chapter provides that knowledge.

Before turning to the activities of this chapter, several notes of orientation are in order. Most important, the activities in this chapter are not intended to teach phonics. Rather, their purpose is preliminary to phonics instruction. The activities in this chapter are intended to lead the children to use their phonemic awareness to build an initial understanding of how the alphabetic principle works. The goal is to introduce the children to the notion that each phoneme is represented by a letter and that the sequence of phonemes that composes a word is represented, left to right, by the sequence of letters that composes its spelling. Again, the activities provided here are preliminary. Their job is to prepare children for instruction in phonics and spelling, not to substitute for such instruction. For an empirically validated alternative that extends further into phonics and spelling, see the kindergarten and first-grade levels of the Open Court program, *Collections for Young Scholars* (1995).

In using these activities, be warned that the children's behaviors must still be monitored carefully. In particular, many children enter school fully aware that learning about print is big business. As a consequence, some will be inclined to completely dismiss their phonemic knowledge in order to concentrate fully on the letters and spellings. Toward discouraging this tendency, most of the games in this chapter are borrowed with minor modification from previous chapters. The familiarity of the games and their play should help to keep the phonemic functions of the letters in the conceptual forefront. In the same spirit, it is wise to switch back to the original, letterless versions of the games from time to time. For convenience, these letterless versions of the games are cited as Reference Activities.

Finally, the activities in this chapter presume that the students have already established a comfortable familiarity with the letters. Just as letter-sound correspondences can't make sense without phonemic awareness, they are unlearnable unless the children can reliably distinguish one letter from another. Ideally, work on naming, recognizing, and printing the letters will have been started early in the year and developed in parallel with the phonological awareness activities. Nevertheless, some of your students are likely to be uncertain with at least some of the letters. Be sure to watch for signs of confusion and provide extra help and practice as needed.

Remember that the core purpose of these activities is to convey to students how the alphabet works. For this reason, the spelling-sound correspondences of all the words to be explored are simple and straightforward. Furthermore, because the emphasis is on *understanding*, we recommend that the number of letters that are introduced be limited to a manageable subset. Based on their phonemic properties and their utility for spelling simple monosyllabic words, we recommend that the focus be on the following letters:

s m d p t n g b r f l (consonants)

a o i u e (short vowels)

Do not worry about introducing additional letters until the students are comfortable with these. Conversely, there is no need to hurry through the entire set as listed above. At this point, building students' ability to work confidently and reflectively with a few letters is far more valuable than rushing to cover some larger number of letters. Furthermore, when the children have grasped the nature of the system, the introduction of new letters will proceed with far greater ease and speed.

REFERENCES

Collections for young scholars. (1995). New York: SRA/McGraw-Hill.

Letters/Spellings

9A 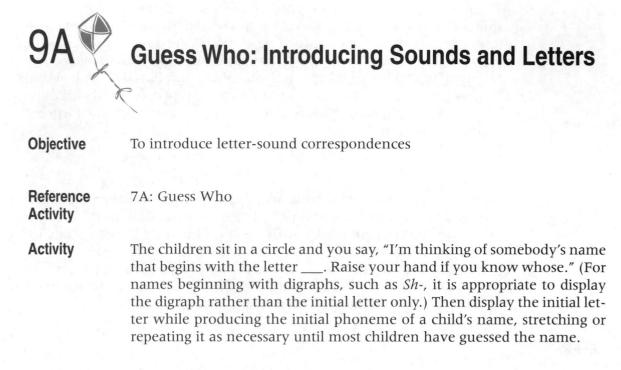 Guess Who: Introducing Sounds and Letters

Objective

To introduce letter-sound correspondences

Reference Activity

7A: Guess Who

Activity

The children sit in a circle and you say, "I'm thinking of somebody's name that begins with the letter ___. Raise your hand if you know whose." (For names beginning with digraphs, such as *Sh-*, it is appropriate to display the digraph rather than the initial letter only.) Then display the initial letter while producing the initial phoneme of a child's name, stretching or repeating it as necessary until most children have guessed the name.

Note: Names beginning with secondary or non-English letter-sound correspondences will require special explanation.

Variation

- After children become familiar with the beginning sounds and letters of each others' names, you may begin the game: "I'm thinking of someone's name that begins with (letter-name)" while displaying the corresponding letter. The children pronounce the sound of the letter and then raise their hands when they have guessed the name of the child.

NOTES AND ADDITIONAL ACTIVITIES

9B  Picture Names: Initial Sounds and Letters

Objective   To pair letters with the initial phonemes of words

Reference Activity   7C: Finding Things: Initial Phonemes

Note: Use this game to introduce each new consonant. It should be played and replayed until the children respond to the focal consonant with reasonable speed and reliability. At that point, the consonant should be reinforced and extended through Activities 9C: I'm Thinking of Something: Initial Sounds and Letters, and 9D: Picture Names: Final Sounds and Letters. Return to this game to introduce the next consonant only when the children are secure with the last.

Move to the sounding and spelling activities (9E: Picture Search: Initial or Final Consonants, 9F: Introduction to How Words Are Spelled: Add a Letter) as soon as the first five consonants have been established. New consonants should continue to be introduced by periodically returning to this activity.

Activity   Use two sets of picture cards. The names of the objects depicted on all the cards in the first set should begin with the letter and phoneme of the day (/s/ on the first day). Those in the second, smaller set of cards begin with some other contrasting sound (/m/ on the first day). Prior to beginning the game, review the name of each picture in the /s/ set with the children so there is no confusion during the game.

Display a picture from the first set and ask the children to name it and identify its initial phoneme (e.g., *socks,* /s-s-s/). Repeat this procedure with a second card from the pile (e.g., *soap,* /s-s-s/).

Then ask, "Do these two words begin with the same sound? What sound do they begin with?" After the children respond, display the letter *s* and say, "This is the letter *s. S* says /s-s-s/. When we write these two words, they both begin with the letter *s.*" The children are then challenged to think of some other word that begins with the same sound; write all that are appropriate on the board, emphasizing that each starts with the letter *s.* Note that because it is only the first letter of the word that is of interest here, inclusion of longer words is fine (e.g., *scissors, sandwich, saxophone*).

    Then shuffle the two sets of cards and display them one at a time so that all can see. For each card, the children are to say *"s"* if the depicted object begins with the sound /s/.

Note: Asking the children to hold up letter cards or tokens as they respond makes it easier for you to monitor their understanding and participation.

Variations

- As a way of assessing individual progress while keeping all engaged, ask the children to refrain from responding until you signal. Then unpredictably call on an individual or the group for the response.

- In the second set of cards, instead of including only pictures that begin with any single other sound, such as /m/, include pictures that begin with a variety of different sounds and letters. This will make the task a bit harder.

- Using picture sets that reflect only two initial letters (e.g., *m* and *s*) challenge the children to identify the initial sound for *every* picture when working through the shuffled cards. Use this variation for reminding children of previously learned letters while working on new ones.

NOTES AND ADDITIONAL ACTIVITIES

9C  I'm Thinking of Something: Initial Sounds and Letters

Objective

To reinforce and extend the children's awareness of each initial consonant by implicitly requiring them to privately name and assess the initial sound of each item they consider during play

Reference Activity

7D: I'm Thinking of Something

Activity

Say, "Now we will play a game called I'm Thinking of Something. I will write down the word I'm thinking of over here. I will give you hints, and you must figure out my word." Write the word someplace where it can be hidden from view during the game and displayed for all to see once it has been guessed.

Then, show and tell the children the initial letter of the word to be guessed. (For this game, initial letters should be restricted to those already introduced.) After presenting the letter, ask the children for its sound: "I'm thinking of something that begins with the letter *s*. What is the sound of the letter *s*?" [/s-s-s/]. Good. Look around the room and see if you see anything that begins with the letter *s*."

Each suggestion made by the children should be reviewed by all to make sure that it does indeed begin with the proper phoneme. When children's suggestions do not begin with the correct sound, draw that observation from the class. Suggestions that do begin with the correct sound should be celebrated and written on the board, emphasizing their initial letter.

Variation

- Play with objects that are not in view by using hints such as "The secret word starts with the letter *s*, it is an animal, it has no legs, it has no fur," and so forth.

9D 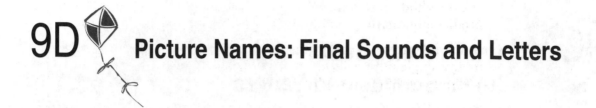 Picture Names: Final Sounds and Letters

Objective   To pair letters with the final phonemes of words.

Note: For each new consonant, it is important that the children be reasonably confident with Activity 9B: Picture Names: Initial Sounds and Letters before challenging them with this activity.

Reference Activity   7G: Different Words, Same Final Phoneme

Activity   Use two sets of picture cards. The names of the objects depicted on all the cards in the first set *end* with the letter and phoneme of the day (/s/ on the first day). Those in the second, smaller set of cards begin with some other contrasting sound (/m/ on the first day). Prior to beginning the game, review the name of each picture in the /s/ set with the children so that there is no confusion about the label to be given as the game is played.

Display a picture from the first set and ask the children to name it and identify its final phoneme (e.g., *dress, /s-s-s/*). Repeat this procedure with a second card from the pile (e.g., *glass, /s-s-s/*). Ask, "Do these two words *end* with the same sound? What sound do they end with?" After the children respond, display the letter *s* and say, "This is the letter *s*. *S* says /s-s-s/. When we write these two words, they both end with the letter *s*." Then write both words on the board to visually emphasize your point.

The children are then challenged to think of some other word that ends with the same sound; acknowledge all that do indeed end with the phoneme in focus. (In cases such as /s/, which is often spelled with a different letter in the ends of words (e.g., *face, palace*), it is best not to write the children's suggestions on the board.)

Then shuffle the two sets of cards and display them one at a time so that all can see. For each card, the children are to say "*s*" if the depicted object ends with the sound /s/. The pictures have been chosen because they, in fact, do end in the focal letter; therefore, they can be written on the board for reinforcement.

Note: Asking the children to hold up letter cards or tokens as they respond makes it easier for you to monitor their understanding and participation.

Variations

- As a way of assessing individual progress while keeping all engaged, ask the children to refrain from responding until you signal. Then unpredictably call on an individual or the group for the response.

- In the second set of cards, instead of including only pictures that end in any single other sound, such as /m/, include pictures that end with a variety of different sounds and letters.

- Using picture sets that reflect only two final letters (e.g., *m* and *s*), challenge the children to identify the initial sound for *every* picture when working through the shuffled cards. Use this variation for reminding children of previously learned letters while working on new ones.

NOTES AND ADDITIONAL ACTIVITIES

9E 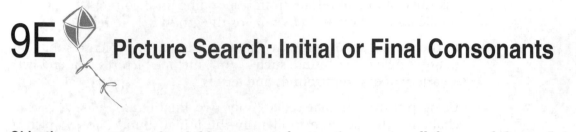 Picture Search: Initial or Final Consonants

Objective　　To get the children to switch attention among all the sounds learned thus far

Note: This game is appropriate only after the children have worked with several letters. Also, because final consonants are harder than initial consonants, they will need more support.

Reference Activities　　7C: Finding Things: Initial Phonemes
　　7H: Finding Things: Final Phonemes

Activities　　For initial consonants, lay out pictures representing each of several letters in the middle of the circle. To play, announce a letter and challenge the children to find a picture that begins with that letter. After an adequate wait-time, ask a child to choose a card and to justify the choice. The child should then remove the picture card from the middle of the circle and line it up under a card showing the corresponding letter. Play the game the same way for final consonants, but ask the children to choose pictures whose names *end* with the consonant you announce.

Variation　　• Pass picture cards out to the children. Each must announce the initial (final) letter of her or his card and add it to the appropriately labeled set.

9F

Introduction to How Words Are Spelled: Add a Letter

Objective   To introduce the children to the left-to-right spellings of words and to the letter-sound correspondences of the short vowels

Note: This activity should be introduced as soon as the children are secure with the first five consonants.

Reference Activities   8B: Basic Three-Sound Words
8C: Consonant Blends: Adding and Subtracting Initial Sounds

Activity   Start by saying a two-sound word (e.g., *at*) and ask the children to segment it for you (e.g., /a/-/t/). Repeating its sounds, write the corresponding letters on the board. Explain that the /a/ sound is represented by the letter *a*. Ask the children to repeat the vowel sound and then to sound and blend the word you have written as you point, left-to-right—first slowly and then quickly—to the letters in turn.

Next, add one of the previously studied letters (e.g., *s*) to the beginning of the word. Ask the children the sound of the new letter and then to figure out the new word by pronouncing and blending the sounds of all three letters that are represented. Until the children have caught on, you will need to model and support this left-to-right sounding and blending activity. After that, the activity is livelier if the children are asked to raise their hands when they know each word and then to justify their response by segmenting it according to the letters and blending it back together again.

The activity proceeds with you making new words by adding or replacing a single letter. After the first day, both initial and final letters should be exercised. Examples of appropriate word sets include:

at	sat	mat	pat		
ad	mad	dad	pad	sad	tad
sa	sat	sad	Sam	sap	
ma	mat	map	man	mad	

New consonants should be added to the activity as soon as they have been introduced, and it is best to stick with the short *a* until a few new consonants have been added to the set. In reintroducing this activity each day and in working through it, care should be taken to reinforce children's attention to the vowel. After the children have become confident with the activity, the short *a* sets should be replaced with short *o* sets. Gradually in this way, each of the short vowels will be introduced and exercised. Revisit each vowel periodically so that the children don't forget one while working with the next.

NOTES AND ADDITIONAL ACTIVITIES

9G   Swap a Letter

Objective   To direct the children's attention to the fact that every letter in a word matters and to develop their appreciation of vowel distinctions

Reference Activities   8C: Consonant Blends: Adding and Subtracting Initial Sounds
8D: Consonant Blends: Inserting and Removing Internal Sounds

Activity   Write a word on the board, and lead the children to sound, blend, and identify it. Then replace one letter of the spelled word. Ask the children to determine the resulting spoken word. Reinforce their response by distinctly sounding and blending its letters. Repeat these steps over and over.

When working with the initial and final consonants, this game is much like the last, only faster paced. When working with vowels, the students will need more support. On any given day, it is best to focus on *one letter position,* either initial, final, or medial (vowel). Examples of appropriate lists include:

Initial:	pot	not	cot	rot	lot	dot	tot
Final:	cat	cap	can	cab			
Medial:	pit	pat	pot	pet			

Again, in order to gain a better sense of the children's confidence and progress, it is a good idea to institute wait-time and to call, unpredictably, on individuals or on the group.

NOTES AND ADDITIONAL ACTIVITIES

9H 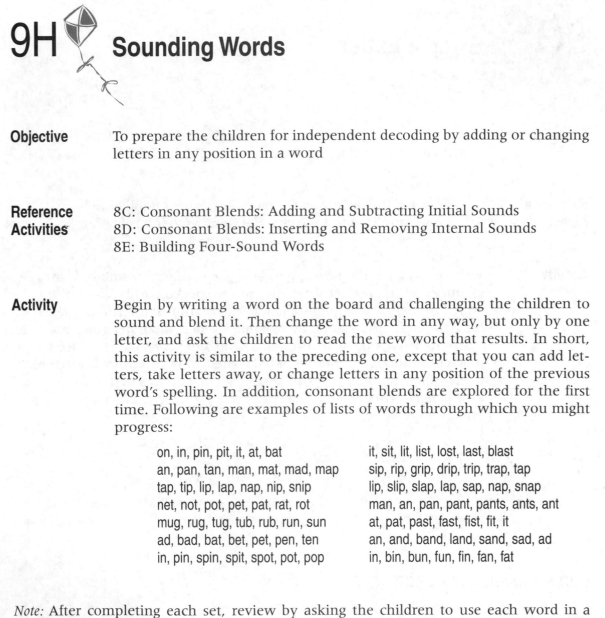 Sounding Words

Objective

To prepare the children for independent decoding by adding or changing letters in any position in a word

Reference Activities

8C: Consonant Blends: Adding and Subtracting Initial Sounds
8D: Consonant Blends: Inserting and Removing Internal Sounds
8E: Building Four-Sound Words

Activity

Begin by writing a word on the board and challenging the children to sound and blend it. Then change the word in any way, but only by one letter, and ask the children to read the new word that results. In short, this activity is similar to the preceding one, except that you can add letters, take letters away, or change letters in any position of the previous word's spelling. In addition, consonant blends are explored for the first time. Following are examples of lists of words through which you might progress:

on, in, pin, pit, it, at, bat
an, pan, tan, man, mat, mad, map
tap, tip, lip, lap, nap, nip, snip
net, not, pot, pet, pat, rat, rot
mug, rug, tug, tub, rub, run, sun
ad, bad, bat, bet, pet, pen, ten
in, pin, spin, spit, spot, pot, pop

it, sit, lit, list, lost, last, blast
sip, rip, grip, drip, trip, trap, tap
lip, slip, slap, lap, sap, nap, snap
man, an, pan, pant, pants, ants, ant
at, pat, past, fast, fist, fit, it
an, and, band, land, sand, sad, ad
in, bin, bun, fun, fin, fan, fat

Note: After completing each set, review by asking the children to use each word in a sentence. Doing so implicitly requires them to reread the words and to consider their meanings.

Variations

- Play an analogous game with writing. Dictate each word and ask the children to write it. After each word and before the next, engage the children in reviewing and troubleshooting their spellings. Celebrate successes and treat the challenge like a brainteaser activity. Use no more than five words on any given day or the game is liable to shift from interesting to arduous.

- Encourage the students to use their phonemic awareness and knowledge of letters to write independently, using inventive or phonetic spellings.

NOTES AND ADDITIONAL ACTIVITIES

10 Assessing Phonological Awareness

This chapter contains assessment procedures for group screening of phonological awareness. Inasmuch as phonology has to do with the sounds of language, paper-and-pencil group testing might seem a bit strange. However, research and experience has demonstrated that such testing can indeed usefully capture young children's general levels of phonological awareness. Meanwhile, in terms of time, group testing is very efficient as compared with individual testing. However, in kindergarten we recommend testing children in groups no larger than six—preferably, in groups of two or three.

By administering the test to everyone in your classroom prior to using the curriculum, you can objectively estimate your students' starting level of phonological awareness. However, for kindergartners it is advised to provide instruction in phonological awareness prior to testing. This pre-assessment is especially valuable for teachers of remedial and primary-grade students, as it provides guidance for adjusting instructional time and effort in accordance with the student's prior knowledge and needs. Although key activities—even from the first chapter of the curriculum—should be sampled to ensure confident understanding by all, work can begin in earnest at the chapter corresponding to the subtest where the students' scores begin to fall off. The assessment can be repeated for all students at intervals of 1–2 months, and the scores can be used to monitor or double-check the progress of the group. Again, lower group scores on any subtest generally indicate that the children should be returned to the corresponding chapter of the curriculum and related activities.

Used properly, the screening can also help you to identify those individuals with phonological difficulties. Here, however, a caveat is in order. Young children often have difficulty with listening to and following directions and, more generally, with the kinds of attention, independence, and metacognitive control that are required by such tests. Despite the fact that this assessment has been designed such that, with support, supervision, and encouragement, most children can meet these demands, individual scores should be treated circumspectly. As a rule of thumb, a high score indicates that a child is progressing well on the capabilities tested. A child may obtain a low score, however, on any or all subtests for reasons wholly unrelated to their content or purpose. Children who perform poorly on any subtest should be further assessed through one-to-one interactions. Where difficulties are affirmed, the child should be given special support until they are conquered (see Torgesen & Bryant, 1994; Wagner & Torgesen, 1997). Bear in mind, too, that a child's performance and confidence in working with relevant games and materials is a more valid indicator of understanding and growth than a score on any small set of test items.

THE ASSESSMENT TEST

The assessment test contains six subtests:

1. Detecting Rhymes
2. Counting Syllables
3. Matching Initial Sounds
4. Counting Phonemes
5. Comparing Word Lengths
6. Representing Phonemes with Letters

The maximum score on each task is 5 points, yielding a total maximum score of 30 points.

MATERIALS

Each child should have a pencil and a test booklet (made by compiling the student testing forms that appear throughout this chapter), including a cover page that is labeled with his or her name. You should have a set of demonstration pages (that appear throughout this chapter), a copy of the student booklet, and a pencil or marker.

THE TESTING PROCEDURE

Administration of the entire test takes about 30 minutes or longer with kindergartners. We recommend that the total size of the tested group not exceed 15 children for first graders and 6 for kindergartners. Larger groups of children tend to be difficult to manage in an assessment situation.

We also recommend that at least two teachers be involved in the administration of the test. Involving another teacher helps to ensure that the children pay attention and follow directions appropriately. In addition, it affords valuable opportunities for discussing the results of the assessment as well as their follow-up implications and strategies.

The following sections provide brief rationales for each subtest and instructions for their administration.

All of the illustrations in this chapter are courtesy of Kathleen Gray Farthing.

DETECTING RHYMES

For most children, the ability to detect and produce rhymes seems to develop without formal instruction. Nevertheless, research shows sensitivity to rhyme to be a useful indicator of a basic, entry level of phonological awareness (Lundberg, Olofsson, & Wall, 1980; Muter, 1994). That is, to appreciate the similarity between the words *hat* and *cat*, the child must shift attention from the meanings of words to the sounds of words. Although solid sensitivity to rhyme does not lead automatically or directly to phonemic awareness, its absence suggests trouble and warrants instructional response.

Description

On the test form, there are 10 pictures. For each picture in the left column, there is another picture on the page with a rhyming name. The children's task is to connect the rhyming pictures by drawing lines between them.

Administration

Begin by explaining that two words rhyme when they sound similar at the end and give the children several examples of rhyming words:

"cheek–peek"
"chair–hair"
"most–toast"

Prompt the children to think of a few more rhymes:

"Can anyone think of a word that rhymes with bed?" (e.g., head, red, bread, said)
". . . with lace?" (e.g., face, race)
". . . with toy?" (e.g., boy, joy)
". . . with king?" (e.g., sing, ring)

Then hold up your demonstration page, which shows two columns of two pictures each, and point to the first picture on the left:

"Can you name this picture?"
"Yes, it is a **clock.** Now look at the pictures on this side of the page. Can you find one that rhymes with **clock?** Raise your hands, if you know."
"Very good, **clock** and **sock** rhyme. Listen: **clock . . . sock.**"
"To show that these two pictures rhyme, I will draw a line between them."

Draw a line between the two pictures to demonstrate, holding up the page to make sure that all see and understand. Then direct the children's attention to the bottom, left picture:

"Here is a picture of a **nail.** Do you see another picture that rhymes with **nail?** Raise your hand if you can."
"Very good, **nail** and **snail** rhyme. Listen: **nail . . . snail.**"
"To show that these two pictures rhyme, I will draw a line between them."

Demonstrate again, making sure all attend.

"Turn to the first page of your booklet. Here you have 10 pictures. Every picture in the left row rhymes with another picture somewhere on the page."

"Find the rhyming words and connect them by drawing a line from one to the other."

"Before you begin, I will tell you the names of the pictures."

Pointing to one picture at a time from top to bottom and left to right, name each clearly, making sure that all children attend and understand:

"Tree, moon, house, cat, car, mouse, hat, spoon, star, bee"

"Okay. Now you start looking for the rhymes. Don't forget to draw a line between pictures that rhyme."

"When you have finished, put down your pencil and look at me."

Scoring

Give each child 1 point for each correctly matched pair so that the maximum possible score is 5.

Detecting Rhymes: Teacher Demonstration Page

Detecting Rhymes: Student Testing Form

COUNTING SYLLABLES

Research shows that the ability to attend to syllables is easier than the ability to attend to phonemes and, furthermore, that syllabic awareness generally emerges earlier than phonemic awareness in the children's development (Lundberg, Frost, & Peterson, 1988). This subtest assesses children's phonemic awareness by asking them to count the number of syllables in different words.

Description

The test form shows five pictures, each followed by a blank response line. The children must indicate the number of syllables in each of the pictured words by writing as many tallies on the response line.

Administration

Begin by showing the children how to count the number of syllables in words. By clapping as you enunciate each syllable, demonstrate words (e.g., *far-mer, nap-kin, sand-wich*) that consist of two syllables. Mark the syllables by clapping hands. Similarly, a few three-syllable words (e.g., *am-bu-lance, bi-cy-cle, ham-bur-ger*) should be clapped and counted. A few monosyllabic words should also be demonstrated (e.g., *book, car, soup*). Then hold up your demonstration page and point to the first picture:

"Look at this picture. What is it?"
"Yes, it is a **window.** Now we say the word slowly and in syllables: **win-dow.**"
"Very good! How many syllables were there?"
"Yes, two. To show that this word has two syllables, we make two marks on the line next to it."

To demonstrate, make two tally marks (| |) on your page. Then pronounce the word *win-dow* once more, pointing to each mark in turn as you enunciate the corresponding syllable. Then direct the children's attention to the next picture on the demonstration page.

"Look at the next picture. What is it?"
"Yes, it's an **alligator.**"
"Let's say this word together slowly, so we can hear the syllables: **al-li-ga-tor.** How many syllables?"
"Yes, four. So what should I do?"
"Yes, I should make four marks in the space next to the alligator."

Demonstrate and display your four tally marks (| | | |). Again, pronounce the word, *alligator,* syllable by syllable, pointing to the four marks in turn as you do so. Now ask the children to look at their test page.

"What do you think you have to do on this page?"
"Yes. For each picture, you must see if you can figure out how many syllables are in the name of each picture you see."
"Before you begin, I will name each picture there."
"Listen carefully: **pencil, elephant, motorcycle, bow, helicopter.**"

"See if you can count the syllables for each picture. Be sure to mark the number of syllables next to each picture."

"When you have finished, put down your pencil and look at me."

Scoring

Give each child 1 point for each correctly identified word so that the maximum possible score is 5.

Counting Syllables: Teacher Demonstration Page

_____

_____

Counting Syllables: Student Testing Form

_____

_____

_____

_____

_____

MATCHING INITIAL SOUNDS

Research shows that the ability to judge whether words have the same first sounds is a critical first step in the development of phonemic awareness. This subtest assesses this ability by asking the children to match items that begin with the same phoneme.

Description

The test form shows 10 pictures. For every picture in the left column, there is exactly one somewhere else on the page that begins with the same phoneme. The children are to connect items that begin with the same sound by drawing a line between them.

Administration

Hold up your demonstration page and point to the top, left picture so that all can see.

"Look at this picture. This is a picture of a **seal.**"
"What is the first sound of the word **seal?** Raise your hand if you know."
"Yes, the first sound of seal is **/s-s-s-s-s/: s-s-s-seal.**"

Now direct the children's attention to the column of pictures on the right side of the page.

"Now look at the pictures on this side of the page. Can you find one that begins with the same first sound as **seal?** If you can, raise your hand."
"Good. **Sun** starts with the same sound as seal. Listen carefully: **s-s-s-sun . . . s-s-s-seal.**"
"Now we draw a line between **seal** and **sun** to show that they begin with the same sound."

Draw a line between the two pictures to demonstrate, holding up the page to make sure that all see and understand. Then direct the children's attention to the bottom, left picture.

"Here is a picture of a **kite.** What is the first sound of the word **kite?** Raise your hand if you know."
"Yes, the first sound of **kite** is **/k/: k-k-kite.**"

Redirect the children's attention to the column of pictures on the right side of the page.

"Do you see a picture over here that begins with the same sound as **kite?**"
"Yes, **king** begins with **/k/.** Listen: **k-k-kite, k-k-king.**"

Draw a line between the two pictures so that all the children can see what you have done. Now ask the children to turn to the test page. Pointing to each column in turn, explain the following:

"For every picture on this side, see if you can find another over here that begins with the same sound."
"When you find two pictures that begin with the same sound, draw a line between them."
"Before you begin, I will tell you the name of each picture."

Point to each picture, top to bottom and left to right, as you name it:

"Listen carefully: **lamp, pig, fork, balloon, heart, bird, feather, hand, leaf, pencil.**"
"Find the pictures that start with the same sound and draw a line between them."
"When you have finished, you can put down your pencil and look at me. Okay, go ahead!"

Scoring

Give each child 1 point for each correctly matched pair so that the maximum possible score is 5.

Matching Initial Sounds: Teacher Demonstration Page

Matching Initial Sounds: Student Testing Form

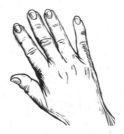

COUNTING PHONEMES

This subtest requires the children to count the number of sounds or phonemes in different words. Research has demonstrated that this task is highly correlated to other tasks on phonemic awareness. It is also a good predictor of reading achievement (Høien, Lundberg, Stanovich, & Bjaalid, 1995).

Description

The test page presents five pictures, each followed by a blank response space. The children are to count the number of phonemes in the words depicted by each picture and to indicate their answers, with tally marks, in the accompanying response space.

Administration

Hold up your demonstration page and point to the first picture:

"Here is a picture of a **knee.** Say the word **knee** very slowly to yourselves. How many sounds do you hear?" (It is the number of phonemes, not the number of letters that is of interest here.)

"Let's try it together. /n/ . . . /ˉe/. How many sounds?"

"Yes, two: /n/ . . . /ˉe/."

"To show that **knee** has two sounds, I have to put two marks here on the line next to its picture."

Making sure that all of the children can see and are paying attention, put two tally marks (I I) next to the picture of a knee on the demonstration page. Then review your solution, pointing to each mark in turn as you voice the phoneme it represents: /n/ . . . /ˉe/.

"What does the next picture show?"

"Yes, the **sun.** How many sounds in the word **sun?**"

"Let's try it together: /s/ . . . /u/ . . . /n/. How many? Good, three. So what should I do next?"

"Good, I have to write three marks in the space next to the sun."

Again making sure that all of the children can see and are paying attention, put three tally marks (I I I) next to the picture of the sun on the demonstration page. Then review, pointing to each mark in turn as you voice the phoneme it represents: /s/ . . . /u/ . . . /n/. Now ask the children to turn to their test page, and continue:

"There are pictures of five things here. You must try to mark how many sounds are in the name of each picture."

"Before you begin, let me name the pictures for you."

Point to each picture in turn while carefully enunciating its name:

"**Toe, ant, broom, soap, paste.**"

"When you figure out the number of sounds in each word, make the same number of marks beside it."

"When you are finished, put down your pencil and look at me."

Scoring

Give each child 1 point for each correct answer so that the maximum possible score is 5.

Counting Phonemes: Teacher Demonstration Page

_____

_____

Counting Phonemes: Student Testing Form

_____

_____

_____

_____

_____

COMPARING WORD LENGTHS

In this task, the children have to compare two words and decide which of them is made up of the greatest number of phonemes. Successful performance requires that the children ignore the meanings of the words, attending only to their phonemic structure.

Description

The test page presents five pairs of pictures. For each set, the children are to circle the picture that represents the word with the greatest number of phonemes.

Administration

Hold up your demonstration page and point to the first pair of pictures:

"Look at the first pair of pictures. One shows a **bow** and the other shows a **boat.** I need to circle the picture that has more sounds. Which of these two pictures should I circle? Raise your hand if you know."

"Let's say both words slowly and compare them: **bow** . . . /b/ . . . /o/. How many sounds does bow have? Yes, two."

"Now let's try **boat:** /b/ . . . /o/ . . . /t/. How many sounds does boat have? Yes, three."

"So which picture should I circle? Which one has more sounds?"

"Yes, boat has more sounds than bow. Listen carefully: **boat . . . bow.**"

Making sure that all are paying attention, circle the picture of the boat. Then repeat the demonstration with the second pair of pictures, *nail* and *snail:*

"Look at the second pair of pictures. One shows a **snail** and the other shows a **nail.** I need to circle the picture that has more sounds. Which of these two pictures should I circle? Raise your hand if you know."

"Let's say both words slowly and compare them: **snail** . . . /s/ . . . /n/ . . . /ā/ . . . /l/. How many sounds does **snail** have? Yes, four."

"Now let's try **nail:** /n/ . . . /ā/ . . . /l/. How many sounds does **nail** have? Yes, three."

"So which picture should I circle? Which one has more sounds?"

"Yes, **snail** has more sounds than **nail.** Listen carefully: **snail . . . nail.**"

Then ask the children to turn to the test page.

"Here are five pairs of pictures. For each pair, you must circle the one that has the most sounds."

"Let me first name them all for you: **card, car; bed, bread; bus, brush; crown, cow; eye, fly.**"

"Remember: for each pair, circle the picture whose name has the most sounds."

Scoring

Give each child 1 point for each correctly marked pair so that the maximum possible score is 5.

Comparing Word Lengths: Teacher Demonstration Page

Comparing Word Lengths: Student Testing Form

REPRESENTING PHONEMES WITH LETTERS

This final task challenges the children to combine their phonemic awareness and letter knowledge to spell words independently. Because it is the children's understanding of the alphabetic principle that is of interest, all of the words involve simple, direct sound-to-letter mappings. Such alphabetic understanding is strongly related to learning to read (Hatcher, Hulme, & Ellis, 1994).

Description

The test form presents five pictures, and the children are asked to spell the name of each.

Administration

Hold up your demonstration page and point to the first picture.

"Here is a picture of a **bat.** Do you think you can spell **bat**? Let's try together."

"Let's start by saying the word **bat** very slowly, sound by sound: **/b/-/a/-/t/.** What is the first sound?"

"So what letter do we write first?"

Making sure all of the children are paying attention, write the letter *b* in the space next to the picture of the bat.

"Okay. What is the second sound of the word **bat.** Listen carefully: **/b/-/a/-/t/.**"

"Which letter do we write for /a/? Good, it's the letter **a.**"

Add the letter *a*. Then, to show that the word is still incomplete, sound what you have spelled thus far as you point to the letters:

"/B/-/a/ . . . That's not enough. What else do we need?"

"Let's listen again: **/b/-/a/-/t/.** Which letter do we write for /t/? Yes, **t.**"

Add the letter *t* and then, left to right as you point to the letters, sound your spelling to show that it is complete and correct. Then ask the children to turn to their test pages. Before asking them to begin, name each of the pictured words for them:

"Sun, mop, pot, frog, nest."

Scoring

Each word should be scored as either correct or incorrect, yielding a maximum possible score of 5 points. Independently of the larger test, the results from this subtest may be rescored for analysis of the children's spelling growth per se. For this purpose, a child should be given 1 point for each sound that is correctly represented, provided that left-to-right order is not violated. As an example, using the word *nest:*

4 points	nest,
3 points	nst, net, nes, nist, nust, nustu
2 points	nset, ns, nt, nat
1 point	n

When scored in this way, the maximum number of points on this subtest is 17. The children's scores should be reviewed to identify any who are significantly behind their classmates so that they can be given extra help.

 _____

Representing Phonemes with Letters: Student Testing Form

_____

_____

_____

_____

_____

INTERPRETING THE RESULTS

Instructions for scoring are given at the end of each subtest. To judge your students' general instructional needs, you must determine their average score for each subtest.

To determine the average score for a subtest, add together the scores from each child who took that subtest and then divide that sum by the total number of children who took the subtest. Bear in mind that the maximum possible score on each subtest is 5.0. If the average score of your students on any given subtest is less than 4.0, the corresponding section of the curriculum should be revisited. If the average score of your students is less than 3.0, the corresponding section of the curriculum warrants more serious attention. Also, find time to sit down with any children whose score falls 2 or more points beneath the class average on any given subtest so that you can discover whether they are indeed in need of extra help and practice.

REFERENCES

Hatcher, P., Hulme, C., & Ellis, A.W. (1994). Ameliorating early reading failure by integrating the teaching of reading and phonological skills: The phonological linkage hypothesis. *Child Development, 65,* 41–57.

Høien, T., Lundberg, I., Stanovich, K.E., & Bjaalid, I.K. (1995). Components of phonological awareness. *Reading and Writing: An Interdisciplinary Journal, 7,* 171–188.

Lundberg, I., Frost, J., & Petersen, O.P. (1988). Effects of an extensive program for stimulating phonological awareness in pre-school children. *Reading Research Quarterly, 33,* 263–284.

Lundberg, I., Olofsson, Å., & Wall, S. (1980). Reading and spelling skills in the first school years predicted from phonemic awareness skills in kindergarten. *Scandinavian Journal of Psychology, 21,* 159–173.

Muter, V. (1994). Influence of phonological awareness and letter knowledge on beginning reading and spelling development. In C. Hulme & M. Snowling (Eds.), *Reading development and dyslexia* (pp. 43–62). London: Colin Whurr.

Torgesen, J.K. (1997). *Comprehensive test of phonological awareness.* Austin, TX: PRO-ED.

Torgesen, J.K., & Bryant, B. (1994). *Phonological awareness training for reading.* Austin, TX: PRO-ED.

Wagner, R.K., & Torgesen, J.K. (1997). *Comprehensive test of phonological processes in reading.* Austin, TX: PRO-ED.

Assessment

A

Phonetic Symbols and Classifications of American English Consonants and Vowels

Table 1. American English consonant phonemes

Phonetic symbol	Phonic symbol	Graphemes for spelling[a]
/p/	/p/	pit, spider, stop
/b/	/b/	bit, brat, bubble
/m/	/m/	mitt, slam, comb
/t/	/t/	tickle, stand, sipped
/d/	/d/	die, loved, handle
/n/	/n/	nice, knight, gnat
/k/	/k/	kite, crlb, quiet, duck, walk
/g/	/g/	girl, Pittsburgh
/ŋ/	/ng/	sing, bank, English
/f/	/f/	fluff, sphere, tough, calf
/v/	/v/	van, dove
/s/	/s/	psychic, pass, science, sit
/z/	/z/	jazz, xerox, zoo, cheese
/θ/	/<u>th</u>/	thin, breath, ether
/ð/	/th/	this, breathe, either
/š/	/sh/	shoe, mission, sure
/ž/	/zh/	measure, azure
/č/	/ch/	cheap, future, etch
/ǰ/	/j/	judge, wage, residual
/l/	/l/	lamb, call, single
/r/	/r/	reach, singer, wrap, car
/j/	/y/	you, use, feud
/w/	/w/	witch, shower, queen
/ʍ/	/wh/	where, when
/h/	/h/	house, who, rehab

Phonetic segment (allophone):

[D]	t, d	writer, ladder, water

From material prepared by Louisa Cook Moats for the Comprehensive Reading Leadership Program, California State Board of Education.

[a]Graphemes are spellings for individual phonemes; those in the word list are among the most common spellings, but the list does not include all possible graphemes for a given consonant.

Table 2. American English consonants (phonic symbols)

	Lips	Lips/ teeth	Tongue between teeth	Tongue behind teeth	Roof of mouth	Back of mouth	Throat
Stop	/p/ /b/			/t/ /d/		/k/ /g/	
Nasal	/m/			/n/		/ng/	
Fricative		/f/ /v/	/th/ /th/	/s/ /z/	/sh/ /zh/		
Affricate					/ch/ /j/		
Glide					/y/	/wh/ /w/	/h/
Liquid				/l/ /r/			

From material prepared by Louisa Cook Moats for the Comprehensive Reading Leadership Program, California State Board of Education.

Table 3.   American English vowels

Phonetic symbol	Phonic symbol	Spellings
/i/	ē	beet
/ɪ/	i	bit
/e/	ā	bait
/ɛ/	e	bet
/æ/	a	bat
/ɑj/	ī	bite
/ɑ/	o	bottle
/ʌ/	u	butt
/ɔ/	aw, ô	bought
/o/	ō	boat
/ʊ/	ŏo	put
/u/	ōo	boot
/ə/	ə	between
/ɔj/	oi, oy	boy
/æω/	ou, ow	bow

From material prepared by Louisa Cook Moats for the Comprehensive Reading Leadership Program, California State Board of Education.

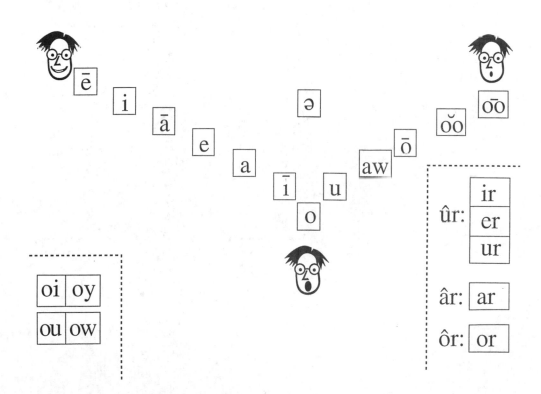

Figure 1.   Vowel spellings by mouth position. (From material prepared by Louisa Cook Moats for the Comprehensive Reading Leadership Program, California State Board of Education.)

B Suggested Kindergarten Schedule

Following is a suggested schedule for progressing through the activities with your kindergarten class. Please remember that this sequence is only a suggestion. Because the activities are sequenced by difficulty, the suggested order should be maintained in introducing them. However, the pace at which they are introduced should be adjusted according to the strengths and needs of your children. As you conduct each activity, you must observe your students carefully to determine the level of interest and understanding of each. Beyond that, the suggested schedule reflects the traditional methodology of introducing, practicing, extending, and revisiting an activity. We recommend that activities be repeated often, even as new activities are being offered. In this way, you will meet the varying needs of your children. As long as you continue to vary the repeated activity and increase its complexity, even the most advanced children will continue to feel interested and challenged. Meanwhile, you will be providing extra practice and reinforcement to those who need it.

In kindergarten, the lessons should be implemented for the duration of the program (which should be about 8 months). On pages 142–143, you will find a black line master for you to reproduce and use in planning and monitoring visits and revisits to the various activities. In this way, you will have a quick visual check of how often each activity is being offered. This, in conjunction with your day-to-day monitoring of your students, should guide you as to when to offer new activities and when to revisit or modify old ones.

Example of Activities for the First 4 Weeks of Work

Day 1	3A Listening to Sounds
	4A Poetry, Songs, and Jingles
Day 2	3A Listening to Sounds
	3B Listening to Sequences of Sounds
	4A Poetry, Songs, and Jingles
Day 3	3B Listening to Sequences of Sounds
	4A Poetry, Songs, and Jingles
	4B Rhyme Stories

Day 4	3B	Listening to Sequences of Sounds
	3C	Jacob, Where Are You?
	4B	Rhyme Stories
Day 5	4A	Poetry, Songs, and Jingles
	3B	Listening to Sequences of Sounds
	3D	Hiding the Alarm Clock
Day 6	3D	Hiding the Alarm Clock
	4A	Poetry, Songs, and Jingles
	3C	Jacob, Where Are You?
Day 7	3E	Who Says What?
	4B	Rhyme Stories
	4C	Emphasizing Rhyme Through Movement
Day 8	4B	Rhyme Stories
	3F	Whisper Your Name
	4C	Emphasizing Rhyme Through Movement
Day 9	4A	Poetry, Songs, and Jingles
	3C	Jacob, Where Are You?
	3E	Who Says What?
Day 10	4A	Poetry, Songs, and Jingles
	3F	Whisper Your Name
	3G	Nonsense
Day 11	3C	Jacob, Where Are You?
	4B	Rhyme Stories
	4A	Poetry, Songs, and Jingles
Day 12	3G	Nonsense
	4B	Rhyme Stories
	4A	Poetry, Songs, and Jingles
Day 13	3H	Whispering Game
	4B	Rhyme Stories
	4C	Emphasizing Rhyme Through Movement
Day 14	3E	Who Says What?
	3I	Do You Remember?
	4A	Poetry, Songs, and Jingles
Day 15	4D	Word Rhyming
	3H	Whispering Game
	4B	Rhyme Stories

Day 16	3F Whisper Your Name
	4A Poetry, Songs, and Jingles
	3G Nonsense

Day 17	4B Rhyme Stories
	4C Emphasizing Rhyme Through Movement
	3I Do You Remember?

Day 18	3F Whisper Your Name
	4B Rhyme Stories
	4D Word Rhyming

Day 19	3G Nonsense
	4A Poetry, Songs, and Jingles
	3C Jacob, Where Are You?

Day 20	3I Do You Remember?
	4D Word Rhyming
	4A Poetry, Songs, and Jingles

Example of Activities After About 10 Weeks of Work

Day 51	4B Rhyme Stories
	5C Hearing Words in Sentences
	6A Clapping Names

Day 52	4A Poetry, Songs, and Jingles
	3H Whispering Game
	4E Can You Rhyme?

Day 53	4B Rhyme Stories
	6A Clapping Names
	4C Emphasizing Rhyme Through Movement

Day 54	4A Poetry, Songs, and Jingles
	5C Hearing Words in Sentences
	4G Action Rhymes

Day 55	4A Poetry, Songs, and Jingles
	5C Hearing Words in Sentences
	3I Do You Remember?

Day 56	4B Rhyme Stories
	4G The Ship Is Loaded with . . .
	5D Exercises with Short and Long Words

Day 57	4A Poetry, Songs, and Jingles
	3G Nonsense
	6B Take One Thing from the Box

Day 58	4B Rhyme Stories
	6A Clapping Names
	5D Exercises with Short and Long Words
Day 59	4A Poetry, Songs, and Jingles
	4G Action Rhymes
	6C The King's/Queen's Successor
Day 60	4B Rhyme Stories
	3I Do You Remember?
	5D Exercises with Short and Long Words

Examples of Activities After About 18 Weeks of Work

Day 91	4H Rhyme Book
	3G Nonsense
	5C Hearing Words in Sentences
Day 92	4B Rhyme Stories
	6A Clapping Names
	7E Word Pairs I: Take a Sound Away (Analysis)
Day 93	7E Word Pairs I: Take a Sound Away (Analysis)
	6D Listening First, Looking After
	5D Exercises with Short and Long Words
Day 94	4B Rhyme Stories
	5E Words in Context and Out
	7F Word Pairs II: Add a Sound (Synthesis)
Day 95	7F Word Pairs II: Add a Sound (Synthesis)
	4H Rhyme Book
	3I Do You Remember?
Day 96	4H Rhyme Book
	7C Finding Things: Initial Phonemes
	7E Word Pairs I: Take a Sound Away (Analysis)
	7F Word Pairs II: Add a Sound (Synthesis)
Day 97	7D I'm Thinking of Something
	6B Take One Thing from the Box
	5C Hearing Words in Sentences
Day 98	4H Rhyme Book
	7F Word Pairs II: Add a Sound (Synthesis)
	3H Whispering Game
Day 99	4B Rhyme Stories
	5E Words in Context and Out
	4G Action Rhymes

Day 100   4H Rhyme Book
                 7D I'm Thinking of Something
                 7G Different Words, Same Final Phoneme

Examples of Activities After About 26 Weeks of Work

Day 131   8A Two-Sound Words
                 4E Can You Rhyme?

Day 132   8A Two-Sound Words
                 8B Basic Three-Sound Words
                 7D I'm Thinking of Something

Day 133   8B Basic Three-Sound Words
                 7G Different Words, Same Final Phoneme
                 4A Poetry, Songs, and Jingles

Day 134   7F Word Pairs II: Add a Sound (Synthesis)
                 8B Basic Three-Sound Words
                 4E Can You Rhyme?

Day 135   7D I'm Thinking of Something
                 8C Consonant Blends: Adding and Subtracting Ini-
                     tial Sounds
                 6A Clapping Names

Day 136   8C Consonant Blends: Adding and Subtracting Ini-
                     tial Sounds
                 8D Consonant Blends: Inserting and Removing
                     Internal Sounds
                 4G Action Rhymes

Day 137   6B Take One Thing from the Box
                 8B Basic Three-Sound Words
                 7H Finding Things: Final Phonemes

Day 138   7F Word Pairs II: Add a Sound (Synthesis)
                 8B Basic Three-Sound Words
                 4B Rhyme Stories

Day 139   8C Consonant Blends: Adding and Subtracting Ini-
                     tial Sounds
                 8D Consonant Blends: Inserting and Removing
                     Internal Sounds
                 7C Finding Things, Initial Phonemes

Day 140   8B Basic Three-Sound Words
                 7I Spider's Web

Black Line Master: Kindergarten

MONTH: _____   MONTH: _____

Dates:

Listening Games

3A Listening to Sounds
3B Listening to Sequences of Sounds
3C Jacob, Where Are You?
3D Hiding the Alarm Clock
3E Who Says What?
3F Whisper Your Name
3G Nonsense
3H Whispering Game
3I Do You Remember?

Rhyming

4A Poetry, Songs, and Jingles
4B Rhyme Stories
4C Emphasizing Rhyme Through Movement
4D Word Rhyming
4E Can You Rhyme?
4F The Ship Is Loaded with...
4G Action Rhymes
4H Rhyme Book

Words and Sentences

5A Introducing the Idea of Sentences
5B Introducing the Idea of a Word
5C Hearing Words in Sentences
5D Exercises with Short and Long Words
5E Words in Context and Out

Awareness of Syllables

6A Clapping Names
6B Take One Thing from the Box
6C The King's/Queen's Successor
6D Listening First, Looking After
6E Troll Talk I: Syllables

Initial and Final Sounds

7A Guess Who
7B Different Words, Same Initial Phoneme
7C Finding Things, Initial Phonemes
7D I'm Thinking of Something
7E Word Pairs I: Take a Sound Away (Analysis)
7F Word Pairs II: Add a Sound (Synthesis)
7G Different Words, Same Final Phoneme
7H Finding Things: Final Phonemes
7I Spider's Web

Phonemes

8A Two-Sound Words
8B Basic Three-Sound Words
8C Consonant Blends: Adding and Subtracting Initial Sounds
8D Consonant Blends: Inserting and Removing Internal Sounds
8E Building Four-Sound Words
8F Guess a Word
8G Troll Talk II: Phonemes

Introducing Letters and Spellings

9A Guess Who: Introducing Sounds and Letters
9B Picture Names: Initial Sounds and Letters
9C I'm Thinking of Something: Initial Sounds and Letters
9D Picture Names: Final Sounds and Letters
9E Picture Search: Initial or Final Consonants
9F Introduction to How Words Are Spelled: Add a Letter
9G Swap a Letter
9H Sounding Words

C Suggested First-Grade Schedule

The following is only a suggestion as to how to schedule the activities. In first grade, the program is implemented in much the same way as in kindergarten, except that the pace is much faster and new activities are introduced more quickly. Just as in kindergarten, you will introduce, practice, extend, and revisit activities. However, it will not be as often or for as long. The length of time you spend with the early activities of listening and rhyming and the concepts of words and sentences will depend on the developmental needs of the children in your class.

As with the kindergarten schedule, these lessons should be implemented on a daily basis of approximately 15 minutes at a regular, pre-designated time of day. For use in the first-grade classroom, however, the duration of the program can be reduced to about 8 weeks as opposed to 8 months in kindergarten. Depending on the entry levels and progress of your students, however, more time may well be needed. In any case, make sure that your students have established a comfortable awareness of phonemes before moving them on to formal reading instruction and phonics; you will not save time by doing otherwise.

For most first graders, you can abbreviate the listening games and move into work with rhymes, jingles, and poetry without delay. If the children have worked with particular rhyming books or poetry in kindergarten, you may want to begin with those. Use of familiar text allows the children to focus on the activity itself. Whatever the focus, choose those games that are most appropriate for your children, but feel free to extend them and make them more complex as needed. You should still adhere, however, to the general sequence of activities.

Day 1	3B Listening to Sequences of Sounds
	3H Whispering Game
	4C Emphasizing Rhyme Through Movement
Day 2	4A Poetry, Songs, and Jingles
	3I Do You Remember?
	4D Word Rhyming

Day 3	4B Rhyme Stories
	5A Introducing the Idea of Sentences
	3G Nonsense
Day 4	5A Introducing the Idea of Sentences
	4A Poetry, Songs, and Jingles
	3I Do You Remember?
Day 5	4B Rhyme Stories
	4E Can You Rhyme?
	5A Introducing the Idea of Sentences
Day 6	5B Introducing the Idea of a Word
	3G Nonsense
	4F The Ship Is Loaded with . . .
Day 7	5B Introducing the Idea of a Word
	4B Rhyme Stories
	4G Action Rhymes
Day 8	5C Hearing Words in Sentences
	3H Whispering Game
	4H Rhyme Book
Day 9	5C Hearing Words in Sentences
	4H Rhyme Book
	4C Emphasizing Rhyme Through Movement
Day 10	5D Exercises with Short and Long Words
	5E Words in Context and Out
	4B Rhyme Stories
Day 11	5D Exercises with Short and Long Words
	4H Rhyme Book
	6A Clapping Names
Day 12	6A Clapping Names
	5E Words in Context and Out
	6B Take One Thing from the Box
Day 13	6B Take One Thing from the Box
	4B Rhyme Stories
	5C Hearing Words in Sentences

Day 14   6D Listening First, Looking After
                          3G Nonsense
                          4H Rhyme Book

Day 15   6D Listening First, Looking After
                          4F The Ship Is Loaded with . . .
                          7A Guess Who

Black Line Master: Grade 1

	Week: ___	Week: ___	Week: ___	Week: ___	Week: ___	Week: ___	Week: ___	Week: ___	Week: ___	Week: ___

Listening Games

3A Listening to Sounds
3B Listening to Sequences of Sounds
3C Jacob, Where Are You?
3D Hiding the Alarm Clock
3E Who Says What?
3F Whisper Your Name
3G Nonsense
3H Whispering Game
3I Do You Remember?

Rhyming

4A Poetry, Songs, and Jingles
4B Rhyme Stories
4C Emphasizing Rhyme Through Movement
4D Word Rhyming
4E Can You Rhyme?
4F The Ship Is Loaded with...
4G Action Rhymes
4H Rhyme Book

Words and Sentences

5A Introducing the Idea of Sentences
5B Introducing the Idea of a Word
5C Hearing Words in Sentences
5D Exercises with Short and Long Words
5E Words in Context and Out

Awareness of Syllables

6A Clapping Names
6B Take One Thing from the Box
6C The King's/Queen's Successor
6D Listening First, Looking After
6E Troll Talk I: Syllables

Initial and Final Sounds

7A Guess Who

7B Different Words, Same Initial Phoneme

7C Finding Things, Initial Phonemes

7D I'm Thinking of Something

7E Word Pairs I: Take a Sound Away (Analysis)

7F Word Pairs II: Add a Sound (Synthesis)

7G Different Words, Same Final Phoneme

7H Finding Things: Final Phoneme

7I Spider's Web

Phonemes

8A Two-Sound Words

8B Basic Three-Sound Words

8C Consonant Blends: Adding and Subtracting Initial Sounds

8D Consonant Blends: Inserting and Removing Internal Sounds

8E Building Four-Sound Words

8F Guess a Word

8G Troll Talk II: Phonemes

Introducing Letters and Spellings

9A Guess Who: Introducing Sounds and Letters

9B Picture Names: Initial Sounds and Letters

9C I'm Thinking of Something: Initial Sounds and Letters

9D Picture Names: Final Sounds and Letters

9E Picture Search: Initial or Final Consonants

9F Introduction to How Words Are Spelled:

   Add a Letter

9G Swap a Letter

9H Sounding Words

Phonemic Awareness in Young Children: A Classroom Curriculum © 1998 by Paul H. Brookes Publishing Co.

D Accompanying Materials and Resources

Before beginning this curriculum with your students, we recommend that you gather the following materials for your classroom. Most are easy to create on your own, and many are available from a number of sources. For convenience, we have parenthetically listed companies from which some of these materials can be purchased.

SPECIALTY ITEMS NEEDED FOR IMPLEMENTING THE ACTIVITIES

☐ Program manual (Paul H. Brookes Publishing Co.)

☐ Animal soundtracks audiotape (Living & Learning, McGraw Hill Children's Publishing)

☐ Soundtrack Games: Soundtracks (Living & Learning, McGraw Hill Children's Publishing)

☐ Pictures that Rhyme Cards (Media Materials) or Word Family Flash Cards (Idea Corporation)

☐ Beginning sounds cards (Media Materials) or Easy Consonants/ Vowels cards (Frank Schaffer Publications, Inc.)

☐ Action Picture Words cards (Frank Schaffer Publications, Inc.)

☐ Set of toy zoo animals

☐ Set of toy farm animals

☐ Beanbag

☐ Sentence strips

☐ Paper bags

☐ Paper crowns

ITEMS USUALLY AVAILABLE IN THE KINDERGARTEN/FIRST-GRADE CLASSROOM OR ELEMENTARY SCHOOL NEEDED FOR IMPLEMENTING THE ACTIVITIES

- ☐ Rhyming books and nursery rhyme books

- ☐ Tape recorder

- ☐ Blocks (unifix) or interlocking cubes or counters

- ☐ Letter cards or magnetic letters

- ☐ Small household items (e.g., boxes, ball of yarn, alarm clock, timer)

- ☐ Magnetic board

OPTIONAL MATERIALS

- ☐ Small mirrors (Local novelty stores or International Dyslexia Association)

- ☐ Alphabet sound teaching tubs (Lakeshore Learning Store)

- ☐ Nursery rhyme posters or pocket chart sets (Creative Teaching Press)

RESOURCES

Creative Teaching Press
10701 Holder Street
Cypress, CA 90630-6017
714-995-7888

McGraw Hill Children's Publishing
8787 Orion Place
Columbus, OH 43240
1-800-417-3261

Frank Schaffer Publications, Inc.
23740 Hawthorne Boulevard
Torrance, CA 90505
310-378-1133

Paul H. Brookes Publishing Co.
Post Office Box 10624
Baltimore, MD 21285-0624
410-337-9580

Lakeshore Learning Store
4050 Thousand Oaks Boulevard
West Lake Village, CA 91362
805-374-6774

World Class Learning Materials,
also called Learning Well
111 Kane Street
Baltimore, MD 21224
410-633-0730

E Advanced Language Games

The following games may be appropriate for the younger child who has completed the original program and is looking for more challenging activities or the older child in special education who has mastered the original activities in kindergarten but continues to need explicit instruction in phonemic awareness to facilitate progress in reading and spelling. Although most are extensions of the original games, there are a few new games. The activities address syllables; initial/final phonemes; and segmenting words into initial, medial, and final phonemes.

Syllable Ball

This game has the format of The Ship Is Loaded with . . . , except that you pronounce a word syllable by syllable and the child responds with the synthesis of the word. For example, say *tel-e-phone,* enunciating the syllables at half-second intervals, and throw a soft ball or beanbag to a child. The child catches the ball and responds with *telephone* while throwing the ball back to you.

Remember to pronounce the syllables as you would in daily speech without regard to spelling. Each of the suggested words has from four to seven syllables. The objective of this game is to help the children understand the nature of syllables and to distinguish them conceptually from words. Use long words to the extent that they are familiar, but intersperse them with shorter (two- and three-) syllable words, which are also quite an important part of the English language. Suggested words include the following:

ca-fe-te-ri-a	ka-lei-do-scope	re-fri-ge-ra-tor
e-lec-tric-i-ty	kin-der-gar-ten	re-spon-si-bil-i-ty
ed-u-ca-tion	math-e-mat-ics	su-per-mar-ket
el-e-va-tor	mo-tor-cy-cle	tel-e-vi-sion
Feb-ru-ar-y	ob-ser-va-tion	ther-mom-e-ter
he-li-cop-ter	per-son-al-i-ty	ty-ran-no-sau-rus
il-lus-tra-tor	pter-o-dac-tyl	

Initial/Final Phonemes: Strange Stories

Alliterative stories and alphabet books provide a wonderful means of introducing and reinforcing initial phonemes of words. When reading aloud, exaggerate the initial sound and have children repeat many of the alliterative words with you. As the children become comfortable with hearing the initial sounds, invite them to compose their own alliterative stories with you. You may want to begin by asking them to compose stories using their own names. Some examples follow:

1. Stephen is sailing his Sunday sail sound around San Francisco's southern tip. The sun is shining so Stephen sweetly sings his silly song.
2. Dennis danced delightful dances daily.
3. Darling Doreen did double duty diving during dessert.
4. Terrible Ted took two tomatoes to Transylvania to tick off two-timing Tina.
5. For fun, Fat Freddy flew five, fine, funky fish from Florida for Father's Friday feast.

Initial Consonant Blends

This game is also played much like The Ship Is Loaded with . . . , except that it uses initial consonant blends. Blends are difficult for most young readers to separate into phonemes, and children in special education may need extra help. Seat the children in a circle. Throw a soft ball or bean-bag to one of the children saying, "The ship is loaded with *s-s-s-n-owballs*," stretching out the initial sound and articulating very clearly the *n* in *-now-balls*. The child catches the ball and offers a new word with the same initial blend; for instance, "The ship is loaded with *s-s-s-n-n-n-akeskins*." Help the child who is having difficulty.

After a few throws, shift to other groups of consonants. A suggested list of words with initial consonant blends follows:

blabbermouth	clams
blackbird	clarinets
blankets	clay
bleach	clerks
blindfold	clocks
blisters	clothes
blockbuster	
blood	crackers
blossoms	cradle
	cranberry
brag	crank
brass	creep
bread	crows
brick	
bride	
brothers	

flags	fractions	slacks	snack
flames	Frankenstein	slap	snails
flamingos	freak	sled	snakeskins
fleas	freckles	sleep	snap
fliers	friends	sleeve	sneakers
flirt	fright	slide	sneeze
float	Frisbee	slingshot	Snickers
flowers	frogs	slinky	snoop
flutes	frown	slipper	snore
		sloppy	snorkels
		slow	snout
		slugs	snowballs

Word Pairs I: Take a Phoneme Away (Analysis)

Prior to doing this activity, reread the description in the original activity on page 64 (Word Pairs I: Take a Sound Away [Analysis]). This game is conducted in much the same way but uses consonant blends and, therefore, is more advanced.

Explain that by taking away sound from a word, one may create a new word. To demonstrate, say *s-s-s-low* with a long, drawn-out initial sound. Have the children repeat in unison. Then say *low*, and again have the children repeat in unison. Then ask which sound has been taken away in the last word. The children are supposed to respond with *s-s-s*. Words with initial consonant blends include the following:

blow–low	stick–tick
snow–no	smile–mile
snail–nail	stop–top
clock–lock	thread–red
click–lick	bread–red
blast–last	drink–rink
broom–room	speak–peek
trip–rip	froze–rose
flight–light	clip–lip
break–rake	blend–lend
cluck–luck	

Word Pairs II: Add a Phoneme

Prior to doing this activity, reread the description in the original activity on page 65 (Word Pairs II: Add a Sound [Synthesis]). This game is conducted in much the same way, but consonant blends are used.

Explain that by adding a sound in front of a word, one may get a new word. As an example, say *ring* and have the children repeat in unison. Explain that now you will add a new sound, /b/ to the front of the word. *b-b-b-ring, bring*. Again, have the children repeat in unison.

As the children become familiar with this process of adding a sound, give them the original word, then the added sound, but ask them what the new word is. The suggested word list for Word Pairs I: Take a Phoneme Away (Analysis) can be used for this activity as well.

I Want

This game trains children to listen for final as well as initial sounds. Say, as an example, "I want a *lollipop*," as you throw a ball or beanbag to a child. That child must respond by naming something she or he wants that begins with the same sound that your wish ended with; for example, "I want a *pumpkin*." The child then throws the ball to another child who must find a word that begins with the sound with which the previous word ended. In this example, the next child must then find a new word that begins with /n/.

Segmenting Words into Initial, Medial, and Final Phonemes: Four- to Seven-Sound Words

This game is played in the same way as the original games with two-, three-, and four-sound words on pages 57–79, except that the words contain consonant blends and, therefore, are much more difficult than the words in the original activities as is apparent from the consonant blend activities on pages 80–87. Example words include the following:

b—r—a—n—ch (branch)
f—l—a—t (flat)
g—r—ee—n (green)
g—r—u—m—p (grump)
p—r—i—s (price)
s—k—oo—l (school)
s—m—i—l (smile)
s—p—r—i—n—t (sprint)
s—t—o—r—k (stork)

Many of the words listed under Initial Consonant Blends on pages 80–81 as well as those listed in the original Word Pairs games (pages 64–65) can also be used for this activity.

Segmentation of Picture Rhymes

Seat the children in a circle. Then hold up a picture and hand it to one child. The child holding the picture must say what it is, articulating the individual sounds in the word, and then think of a word that rhymes with it; for example, given a picture of a house, the child might say, /h/-/ow/-/s/ . . . /m/-/ow/-/s/. Remember that for these activities it is the sounds, not the spellings, that are important. (*Note:* Many children will want to segment the word into its onset-rhyme, rather than into separate phonemes. For example, house–mouse becomes /h/–/ouse/ . . . /m/–/ouse/ at the onset-rhyme level. Praise such responses and proceed to demonstrate how the rhyming words can be broken down even further into phonemes.)

Guess a Word

Select several pictures that represent many different sounds, and then seat the children in a circle. The pictures chosen will depend on how advanced the class is (the more advanced, the more sounds in the words represented by the pictures). Then take a "secret" picture out and give it to one of the children, telling him or her to peek at it but not to let anyone else see it. Then, ask the child to sound out all of the phonemes in the word pictured, with clear pauses between each phoneme. The other children must now figure out what the word is. (*Note:* Careful modeling of the activity is important for the children to be able to understand what is expected.)

Troll Talk III: Phonemes and Blends

This game is played in much the same way as Troll Talk I and II (on pages 56 and 89) but with more complex words, for instance, words with consonant blends.

F ✦ **Annotated Bibliography of Rhyming Stories**

Aardema, V. (1981). *Bringing the rain to Kapiti Plain*. New York: The Dial Press.

Ahlberg, J. (1979). *Each peach pear plum*. New York: Viking. Rhymed text and illustrations invite the reader to play I Spy with a variety of Mother Goose and other folklore characters.

Alborough, J. (1992). *Where's my teddy?* Cambridge, MA: Candlewick Press. When a small boy named Eddie goes searching for his lost teddy in the dark woods, he comes across a gigantic bear with a similar problem.

Alda, A. (1992). *Sheep, sheep, sheep, help me fall asleep*. New York: Bantam Doubleday Dell Books for Young Readers. It's bedtime and once Mom leaves the room, this preschooler who isn't ready to fall asleep counts not just sheep but other animals doing a variety of things.

Alda, A. (1994). *Pig, horse, cow, don't wake me now*. New York: Bantam Doubleday Dell Books for Young Readers. Playful verse describes a young child and young animals who need some coaxing to wake up in the morning.

Bayer, J. (1984). *A my name is Alice*. New York: The Dial Press. Through lively alliteration, a different character for each letter of the alphabet is described in terms of name, place he or she lives, and occupation.

Berenstain, S., & Berenstain, J. (1988). *The Berenstain bears and the ghost of the forest*. New York: Random House, Inc. Papa Bear's attempt to scare a band of young campers by telling them about ghosts in the woods comes to an unexpected conclusion with a double ghost lesson.

Brown, M. (1994). *Pickle things*. New York: Parents Magazine Press. Describes, in rhymed text and illustrations, all the many things that a pickle isn't.

Brown, M.W. (1989). *Goodnight moon*. New York: Scholastic.

Brown, M.W. (1993). *Four fur feet*. New York: Bantam Doubleday Dell Books for Young Readers. As the "four fur feet" of this furry animal travel around the world, children are drawn into the pattern repeated in every sentence and the simple descriptions of this furry animal's travels.

Bucknall, C. (1985). *One bear all alone*. New York: The Dial Press. Relates the activities of one to ten bears during a busy day.

Bunting, E. (1991). *In the haunted house*. New York: Clarion Books. A little girl and her father tour a dark, mysterious house, which is eventually revealed to be a "Halloween House."

Butler, J., & Schade, S. (1998). *I love you, good night*. New York: Simon & Schuster. A mother and child tell each other how much they love each other at bedtime through rhyming language play such as the child saying she loves her mother as much as "blueberry pancakes" and the mother responding with she loves the child as much as "milkshakes."

Cameron, P. (1961). *"I can't," said the ant*. New York: Coward-McCann. Ant struggles in vain to rescue the teapot from the kitchen floor, but with the help of friends, Miss Teapot is finally saved.

Capucilli, A. (1993). *Inside a barn in the country*. New York: Scholastic. One after another, the animals in a barn wake each other up with the unique sounds they make.

Carle, E. (1974). *All about Arthur (an absolutely absurd ape)*. New York: Franklin-Watts. Arthur, an accordion-playing ape, travels from city to city making friends whose names begin with the same initial sound of the city in which they live such as "Young Yak in Yonkers."

Carter D. (1990). *More bugs in boxes*. New York: Simon & Schuster. This pop-up book uses alliteration to ask and answer questions about the make-believe bugs found inside of a series of boxes.

Chapman, C. (1993). *Pass the fritters, critters*. New York: Four Winds Press. Hungry animals passing food during a meal learn that "please" is a magic word.

Cole, J. (1989). *Anna Banana: 101 jump rope rhymes*. New York: Morrow Junior Books. A collection of 101 jump rope rhymes arranged and illustrated according to the type of jump rope skill required.

Cooper, M. (1993). *I got a family*. New York: Holt, Rinehart & Winston. In rhyming verses, a young girl describes how the members of her family make her feel loved.

de Regniers, B., Moore, E., White, M., & Carr, J. (1988). *Sing a song of popcorn*. New York: Scholastic. A collection of poetry of well-loved poets from the classic to the contemporary, all beautifully illustrated by Caldecott medal artists.

Degen, B. (1983). *Jamberry*. New York: Harper & Row. A little boy walking in the forest meets a big lovable bear that takes him on a delicious berry-picking adventure in the magical world of Berryland.

Deming, A.G. (1994). *Who is tapping at my window?* New York: Penguin. Through rhyming of animal names, a child tries to discover who is tapping at her window.

Dodds, D.A. (1992). *The color box*. Boston: Little, Brown. Alexander the monkey finds an ordinary-looking box with spots of color inside through which he journeys to many bright landscapes of different colors. Each page has a hole revealing the next color he will find.

Ehlert, L. (1989). *Eating the alphabet: Fruits and vegetables from A to Z*. San Diego: Harcourt Brace Jovanovich. Brightly colored pictures of fruits and vegetables are offered for each letter of the alphabet.

Ehlert, L. (1993). *Nuts to you*. San Diego: Harcourt Brace Jovanovich. A rascally squirrel has an indoor adventure in a city apartment.

Emberley, B. (1992). *One wide river to cross*. Boston: Little, Brown. Through rhyming verse, the gathering of the animals on the ark when the rain began is described, in this adaptation of the African American spiritual about Noah's Ark.

Fleming, D. (1991). *In the tall, tall grass*. New York: Holt, Rinehart & Winston. Rhymed text (crunch, munch, caterpillar's lunch) presents a toddler's view of creatures found in the grass from lunchtime till nightfall, such as bees, ants, and moles.

Fleming, D. (1993). *In the small, small pond*. New York: Holt, Rinehart & Winston. Illustrations and rhyming text describe the activities of animals living in and near a small pond as spring progresses to autumn.

Fleming, D. (1994). *Barnyard banter*. New York: Holt, Rinehart & Winston. All the farm animals are where they should be, clucking and mucking, mewing and cooing, except for the missing goose.

Florian, D. (1987). *A winter day*. New York: Greenwillow Books. A family enjoys a winter day of relaxation and fun.

Florian, D. (1994). *The beast feast*. New York: Scholastic. Each poem in this collection describes a different "beast" in rhyming verse.

Fortunata. (1968). *Catch a little fox*. New York: Scholastic. A group of children are planning a hunting trip describing in rhyming verse the animals they will catch and where they will keep them.

Fox, M. (1993). *Time for bed*. San Diego: Harcourt Brace Jovanovich. A wonderful bedtime story in verse as one young animal after another is put to sleep, with the last one being a child saying "Goodnight."

Galdone, P. (1968). *Henny Penny*. New York: Scholastic. This classic story using rhyming names for the characters describe Henny Penny running from place to place to alert the king and her friends that the sky is falling.

Geraghty, P. (1992). *Stop that noise!* New York: Crown. A mouse is annoyed with the many sounds of the forest until she hears a bulldozer felling trees.

Gordon, J. (1991). *Six sleepy sheep*. New York: Puffin Books. As six sheep try to fall asleep, they go through a variety of antics such as telling spooky stories and sipping soup, all activities beginning the letter *s*.

Greene, C. (1983). *The thirteen days of Halloween*. Chicago: Childrens Press. A Halloween version of "The Twelve Days of Christmas," featuring such seasonal gifts as bats, gobblins, spiders, worms, and ghosts.

Grossman, B. (1995). *The banging book*. New York: HarperCollins. Some very noisy children discover that building things by banging is much more rewarding than tearing things apart.

Grossman, B. (1996). *My little sister ate one hare*. New York: Crown. Little sister has no problem eating one hare, two snakes, and three ants; but when she gets to ten peas, she throws up quite a mess.

Guarino, D. (1989). *Is your mama a llama?* New York: Scholastic. A young llama asks his friends if their mammas are llamas and finds out, in rhyme, that their mothers are other types of animals.

Hague, K. (1984). *Alphabears*. New York: Henry Holt & Co. In this beautifully illustrated book, the special qualities of bears named for each letter of the alphabet are described in rhyme.

Hague, M. (1993). *Teddy bear, teddy bear: A classic action rhyme*. New York: Morrow Junior Books. An illustrated version of the traditional rhyme that follows the activities of a teddy bear.

Hawkins, C., & Hawkins, J. (1983). *Pat the cat*. New York: G.P. Putnam's Sons. Hawkins, C., & Hawkins, J. (1984). *Mig the pig*. New York: G.P. Putnam's Sons. Hawkins, C., & Hawkins, J. (1985). *Jen the hen*. New York: G.P. Putnam's Sons. Hawkins, C., & Hawkins, J. (1986). *Tog the dog*. New York: G.P. Putnam's Sons. In this series of books that focus on changing beginning letters while maintaining the spelling pattern throughout the story, children develop phonemic awareness and familiarity with common spelling patterns.

Heller, R. (1981). *Chickens aren't the only ones*. New York: Grosset & Dunlap. A pictorial introduction to the animals that lay eggs, including chickens as well as other birds, reptiles, amphibians, fishes, and even a few mammals.

Hennessy, B.G. (1989). *The missing tarts*. New York: Viking. When the Queen of Hearts discovers that her strawberry tarts have been stolen, she enlists the help of many popular nursery rhyme characters in order to find them.

Hennessy, B.G. (1991). *Eeney, Meeney, Miney, Mo*. New York: Viking. Eeeney, Meeney, Miney, and Mo take a romp through the jungle, collecting animals as they go along.

Hoberman, M.A. (1982). *A house is a house for me*. New York: Puffin Books. Lists in rhyme the dwellings of various animals and things.

Hutchins, P. (1976). *Don't forget the bacon*. New York: Mulberry. In this book of rhyming and language play, a boy is going to the market for his mother and brings back all of the wrong items.

Hymes, L., & Hymes, J. (1964). *Oodles of noodles*. New York: Young Scott Books. In this collection of poems, words both rhyme and make use of the same initial sounds in order to create nonsense words to complete the verse.

Johnston, T. (1991). *Little bear sleeping*. New York: G.P. Putnam's Sons. In this story told in verse, a yawning bear tries to convince his mother that it isn't time for bed.

Jorgensen, G. (1988). *Crocodile beat*. New York: Scholastic. A crocodile lies by the river awaiting his prey as many other animals come down to the river to play.

Komaiko, L. (1987). *Annie Bananie*. New York: Harper & Row. Sad because her best friend, Annie Bananie, is moving away, a little girl remembers all the fun they had together.

Komaiko, L. (1988). *Earl's too cool for me*. New York: Harper & Row. The antics and adventures of the cool boy Earl include riding on the Milky Way, growing a rose from his fingernails, and swinging with gorillas.

Krauss, R. (1985). *I can fly*. New York: Golden Press. Described in rhyme, a child imitates the actions of a variety of animals.

Kuskin, K. (1990). *Roar and more*. New York: Harper Trophy. Through poems and pictures, a child's attention is brought to the sounds that animals make.

Lerner, S. (1985). *Big Bird says ___: A game to read and play*. New York: Random House. Sesame Street Muppet characters play a game in which they obey commands from Big Bird.

Lewison, W. (1992). *Buzz said the bee*. New York: Scholastic. As an animal tower is being built, each animal does something that rhymes with the animal he will be climbing on top of, for example, "The hen dances a jig before sitting on the pig."

Lindbergh, R. (1990). *The day the goose got loose*. New York: The Dial Press. The day the goose gets loose, havoc reigns at the farm as the animals react.

Martin, B. (1974). *Sounds of a pow-wow*. New York: Holt, Rinehart & Winston. A collection of songs for children to share, some of which use alliteration.

Martin, B., & Archambault, J. (1986). *Barn dance!* New York: Holt, Rinehart & Winston. Unable to sleep on the night of a full moon, a young boy follows the sound of music across the fields and finds an unusual barn dance in progress.

Martin, B., & Archambault, J. (1987). *Here are my hands*. New York: Holt, Rinehart & Winston. The owner of a human body celebrates it by pointing out various parts and mentioning their functions, from "hands for catching and throwing" to the "skin that bundles me in."

Martin B., & Archambault, J. (1988). *Up and down on the merry-go-round*. New York: Henry Holt & Co. In this rhyming story, children describe the sights and sounds of riding on the merry-go-round.

Martin, B., & Archambault, J. (1989). *Chicka chicka boom boom*. New York: Simon & Schuster. An alphabet rhyme/chant that relates what happens when the whole alphabet tries to climb a coconut tree.

Martin, B., & Carle, E. (1991). *Polar bear, polar bear, what do you hear?* New York: Simon & Schuster Books for Young Readers. Zoo animals from a polar bear to walrus make their distinctive sounds for each other while children imitate the sounds for the zookeeper.

Martin, L. (1993). *When dinosaurs go visiting*. New York: Scholastic. The preparations and festivities involved in a dinosaur family going on a visit are described in rhyming verse.

Marzollo, J. (1989). *The teddy bear book*. New York: The Dial Press. A collection of songs, rhymes, jump rope chants, poems, cheers, and story poems honors the teddy bear through the use of rhyming.

Marzollo, J. (1994). *Ten cats have hats*. New York: Scholastic. Pictures and rhyming text present animals from one bear to ten cats with their assorted possessions.

McKissack, P., & McKissack, F. (1988). *Bugs!* Chicago: Childrens Press. Simple text and illustrations of a variety of insects introduce the numbers 1 through 5.

McPhail, D. (1993). *Pigs aplenty, pigs galore*. New York: Dutton Children's Books. Pigs galore invade a house and have a wonderful party.

Medearis, A.S. (1991). *Dancing with the Indians*. New York: Holiday House. While attending a Seminole Indian celebration, an African American family watches and joins in several exciting dances.

Miranda, A. (1996). *Pignic: An alphabet book in rhymes*. Honesdale, PA: Boyds Mill Press. Pigs gather for their annual picnic in this rhyming alphabet book.

Neitzel, S. (1989). *The jacket I wear in the snow*. New York: Greenwillow Books. A young girl names all the clothes that she must wear to play in the snow.

Neitzel, S. (1992). *The dress I'll wear to the party*. New York: Greenwillow Books. In cumulative verses and rebuses, a girl describes how she is dressing up in her mother's party things.

Nerlove, M. (1989). *Hanukkah*. Niles, IL: A. Whitman. Rhyming text and illustrations follow the activities of a little boy and his parents as they prepare to celebrate Hanukkah.

Obligado, L. (1983). *Faint frogs feeling feverish and other terrifically tantalizing tongue twisters*. New York: Viking. A verse for each letter of the alphabet is presented using tongue twisters and alliteration.

Ochs, C.P. (1991). *Moose on the loose*. Minneapolis, MN: Carolrhoda Books. A zookeeper runs through the town looking for a "moose on the loose," and each person he asks has not seen the moose but has seen a different animal, such as a "pig wearing a wig."

Oppenheim, J. (1989). *Not now! said the cow*. New York: Bantam Books. In this story based on "The Little Red Hen," a little black crow asks his animal friends to help with the planting of some corn seed.

Oppenheim, J. (1991). *Eency weency spider*. New York: A Byron Preiss Book. After climbing the water spout, eency weency spider meets Little Miss Muffet, Humpty Dumpty, and Little Jack Horner.

Oppenheim, J. (1993). *"Uh-oh!" said the crow*. New York: Bantam Books. On a dark and windy night, the animals in the barn are frightened by strange noises above them and think there might be a ghost in the barn with them.

Otto, C. (1991). *Dinosaur chase*. New York: Harper Trophy. Both alliteration and rhyme are used in this story of a mother dinosaur reading to her little one about dinosaurs who "crawl, creep, tiptoe, and seek."

Parry, C. (1991). *Zoomerang-a-boomerang: Poems to make your belly laugh*. A collection of silly poems playing with language.

Patz, N. (1983). *Moses supposes his toeses are roses*. San Diego: Harcourt Brace Jovanovich. A variety of language play including assonance, rhyming, alliteration, and tongue twisters engage the reader in this fun collection of seven rhymes.

Philpot, L., & Philpot, G. (1993). *Amazing Anthony ant*. New York: Random House. Based on the old favorite tune "The Ants Go Marching," this book follows Anthony the Ant through a maze as the reader sings and lifts flaps that give clues to help Anthony find his way.

Pilkey, D. (1990). *'Twas the night before Thanksgiving*. New York: Orchard Books. School children on a field trip to Mack Nugget's farm save the lives of eight turkeys in this poem based on "The Night Before Christmas."

Pomerantz, C. (1974). *The piggy in the puddle*. New York: Macmillan. Unable to persuade a young pig from frolicking in the mud, her family finally joins her for a mud party.

Pomerantz, C. (1993). *If I had a paka*. New York: Mulberry. The author manipulates words and plays with language in this collection of poems representing 12 languages.

Prelutsky, J. (1983). *It's Valentine's Day*. New York: Greenwillow Books. A collection of Valentine poems including "I Made My Dog a Valentine" and "I Love You More Than Applesauce."

Prelutsky, J. (1988). *Tyrannosaurus was a beast: Dinosaur poems*. New York: Greenwillow Books. A collection of humorous poems about dinosaurs.

Prelutsky, J. (1989). *Poems of A. Nonny Mouse*. New York: Alfred A. Knopf. In this fun collection of poems and tongue twisters, A. Nonny Mouse gets credit for all the works previously credited to Anonymous.

Prelutsky, J. (1992). *The baby Uggs are hatching*. New York: Mulberry. Using both rhyming and alliteration, these 12 poems describe the activities of many unusual creatures.

Provenson, A., & Provenson, M. (1977). *Old Mother Hubbard*. New York: Random House. In this adaptation of the traditional rhyme, Old Mother Hubbard returns from each of her errands to find her dog doing some activity to rhyme with the errand, for example, she returns from "buying a wig" to find him "dancing a jig."

Raffi. (1987). *Down by the bay*. New York: Crown. In this song, Mother asks her son, "Did you ever see a goose kissing a moose, a fly wearing a tie, or llamas eating pajamas down by the bay?"

Raffi. (1989). *Tingalayo*. New York: Crown. In this book written to make children laugh, a man calls for his Tingalayo and describes his antics in rhyme and rhythm.

Rogers, P. (1990). *What will the weather be like today?* New York: Greenwillow Books. Animals and humans discuss, in rhyming verse, the possibilities of the day's weather.

Rothman, J. (1979). *This can lick a lollipop: Body riddles for kids*. Garden City, NY: Doubleday. Presents riddles in rhyme about various parts of the human body (both Spanish and English texts available).

Sendak, M. (1990). *Alligators all around: An alphabet*. New York: Harper Trophy. Sendak uses alliteration for each letter of the alphabet to introduce the reader to alligators who have headaches (H) and keep kangaroos (K).

Serfozo, M. (1988). *Who said red?* New York: M.K. McElderry Books. A dialogue between two speakers, one of whom must keep insisting on an interest in the color red, introduces that hue as well as green, blue, yellow, and others.

Seuss, Dr. (1960). *One fish, two fish, red fish, blue fish*. New York: Beginner Books. A story-poem about the activities of such unusual animals as the Nook, Wump, Yink, Yop, Gack, and the Zeds.

Seuss, Dr. (1965). *Fox in socks*. New York: Random House. Tricky language play with subtle vowel changes is the focus of this fun book as the fox tries to trip up the reader's tongue.

Seuss, Dr. (1972). *In a people house*. New York: Random House. Easy-to-read rhyme cites a number of common household items.

Seuss, Dr. (1974). *There's a wocket in my pocket*. New York: Random House. A child talks about the nonsense creatures he has found around the house ("grush on my brush") in this wonderful book of language play, which substitutes the initial sounds of common household objects to create the nonsense.

Seuss, Dr. (1991). *Dr. Seuss's ABC's* (2nd ed.). New York: Random House. The antics of many silly nonsense characters are described in alliteration with a different character representing each letter of the alphabet.

Shaw, N. (1986). *Sheep in a jeep*. Boston: Houghton Mifflin. Rhyming verse is used to record the crazy adventures of a group of sheep that go riding in a jeep.

Shaw, N. (1989). *Sheep on a ship*. Boston: Houghton Mifflin. Using rhyming and alliteration, this book describes the adventures of some sheep that go on a trip aboard a ship.

Sheppard, J. (1994). *Splash, splash*. New York: Macmillan. All kinds of animals from a bee to a frog fall into the water, making their own distinctive noises as they fall in the water and get wet.

Showers, P. (1961). *The listening walk*. New York: HarperCollins. A little girl and her father take a walk and identify the sounds around them.

Silverstein, S. (1964). *A giraffe and a half*. New York: HarperCollins. In this cumulative story, Silverstein builds the story of a giraffe using rhyming verses to describe the giraffe and then reverses the events.

Simmonds, P. (1995). *F-freezing ABC's*. New York: Alfred A. Knopf. An anteater, a bear, a cat, and a duck all search for a warm place to stay.

Speed, T. (1995). *Two cool cows*. New York: Scholastic. A modern adaptation of the traditional nursery rhyme, "Hey Diddle Diddle," finds these two cool cows trying to get to the moon.

Staines, B. (1989). *All God's critters got a place in the choir*. New York: Penguin. This book uses rhyme to describe the place that each of God's animals has in the world's choir.

Tallon, R. (1979). *Zoophabets*. New York: Scholastic. Lively alliteration describes a fictional animal for each letter of the alphabet, including where it lives and what it eats.

Van Allsburg, C. (1987). *The Z was zapped*. Boston: Houghton Mifflin. Each letter of the alphabet is involved in some alliterative misfortune such as "B is badly bitten."

Van Laan, N. (1990). *A mouse in my house*. New York: Alfred A. Knopf. One house seems to contain an entire menagerie of active animals, which get into all kinds of mischief and trouble; but in the end they are all found to be the young narrator.

Van Rynbach, I. (1995). *Five little pumpkins*. Honesdale, PA: Boyds Mill Press. The traditional finger rhyme illustrated with lively watercolors.

Wells, R. (1973). *Noisy Nora*. New York: The Dial Press. Feeling neglected, Nora makes more and more noise to attract her parents' attention.

Westcott, N.B. (1988). *The lady with the alligator purse*. Boston: Little, Brown. The jump rope/nonsense rhyme features an ailing young Tiny Tim.

Williams, S. (1990). *I went walking*. San Diego: Harcourt Brace Jovanovich. During the course of a walk, a young boy identifies animals of different colors.

Winthrop, E. (1986). *Shoes*. New York: Harper Trophy. A look at many different kinds of shoes through the use of rhyme and rhythm.

Wood, A. (1992). *Silly Sally*. San Diego: Harcourt Brace Jovanovich. A rhyming story of Silly Sally, who makes many friends as she travels into town, backward and upside down.

Yolen, J. (1987). *The three bears rhyme book*. San Diego: Harcourt Brace Jovanovich. Fifteen poems portray three familiar bears and their friend Goldie engaged in such activities as taking a walk, eating porridge, and having a birthday party.

Young, R. (1992). *Golden bear*. New York: Viking. Golden bear and his human companion learn to play the violin, talk to a ladybug, make mudpies, wish on stars, and dream together.

Zemach, M. (1976). *Hush, little baby*. New York: E.P. Dutton. In this traditional rhyming lullaby, parents attempt to quiet a crying baby through the promise of many things, including a mockingbird, diamond, billy goat, and others.

Ziefert, H., & Brown, H. (1996). *What rhymes with eel?* New York: Penguin. In this simple word and picture flap book, rhyming words are tied to rhyming pictures, allowing children to predict what is under the flap.

G Poems, Fingerplays, Jingles, and Chants

Jack Be Nimble

Jack be nimble. Jack be **quick,**
Jack jump over the **candlestick.**

Jack be nimble, quick as a **fox,**
Jack jump over this little **box.**

Jack be nimble. Jack cut a **caper.**
Jack jump over this little piece of **paper.**

Jack be nimble. Jack be **fair,**
Jack jump over this little **chair.**

Jack be nimble and bright as a **star,**
Stand up and jump very wide and **far.**

This Old Man

This old man, he can **shake,**
Shake, shake, shake while baking a **cake,**
Nick nack paddy wack, give your dog a bone,
Shaking, shaking all the way home.

This old man, he can **kick,**
Kick, kick, kick, kick just for a **trick,**
Nick nack paddywack, give your dog a bone,
Kicking, kicking all the way home.

This old man, he can **twist,**
Twist, twist, twist while shaking his **fist,**
Nick, nack paddywack, give your dog a bone,
Twisting, twisting all the way home.

"Jack be Nimble," "This Old Man," "Reaching with my Arms," and "Rocking Boat" are from Cherry, C. (1971). *Creative movement for the developing child*. Belmont, CA: Fearon Publishers; reprinted by permission.

This old man, he can **sway,**
Sway, sway, sway while trying to **play,**
Nick, nack paddywack, give your dog a bone,
Swaying, swaying all the way home.

This old man, he can **point,**
Point, point, point all over the **joint,**
Nick, nack paddywack, give your dog a bone,
Pointing, pointing, all the way home.

This old man, he can **run,**
Run, run, run, run just for **fun,**
Nick nack paddywack, give your dog a bone,
Running, running all the way home.

This old man, he can **slide,**
Slide, slide, slide from side to **side,**
Nick nack paddywack give your dog a bone,
Sliding, sliding all the way home.

This old man, he can **jump,**
Jump, jump, jump, jump over a **bump,**
Nick, nack paddywack, give your dog a bone,
Jumping, jumping all the way home.

Reaching with my Arms

I reach with my one arm, then with the **other,**
I reach for my sister, I reach for my **brother,**
I reach for the ceiling, I reach for the **wall,**
I reach for so many things, I reach for them **all.**

Rocking Boat

Did you ever see a rocking boat,
On its back so **flat?**
Hands holding onto its knees,
And staying just like **that.**
Then arock and arock and arock, rock, rock,
All across the **sea,**
Arock and arock and arock, rock, rock.
Rock along with **me.**

Did you ever see a rocking boat,
On its tummy **flat?**
Hands in front and feet in back,
And staying just like **that.**
Then arock, and arock, and arock, rock, rock,
All across the **sea,**

Arock and arock and arock, rock, rock,
Rock along with **me.**

Did you ever see a rocking boat,
On its tummy **flat?**
Hand holding onto its feet,
And staying just like **that.**
Then arock and arock and arock, rock, rock,
All across the **sea,**
Arock and arock and arock, rock, rock, rock,
Rock along with **me.**

One, Two, How Do You Do?

1, **2,** how do you **do?**
1, 2, **3,** clap with **me.**
1, 2, 3, **4,** jump on the **floor.**
1, 2, 3, 4, **5,** look bright and **alive.**
1, 2, 3, 4, 5, **6,** your shoe to **fix.**
1, 2, 3, 4, 5, 6, **7,** look up to **heaven.**
1, 2, 3, 4, 5, 6, 7, **8,** draw a round **plate.**
1, 2, 3, 4, 5, 6, 7, 8, **9,** get in **line.**

Stretch Up High

Stretch, stretch away up high, (Reach arms upward)
On your tiptoes, reach the sky, (Stand on tiptoes and reach)
See the bluebirds flying high. (Wave hands)
Now bend down and touch your toes, (Bend to touch toes)
Now sway as the North Wind blows. (Move body back and forth)
Waddle as the gander goes. (Walk in waddling motion)

Two Little

Two little feet go tap, tap, tap
Two little hands go clap, clap, clap
A quiet little leap up from my chair
Two little arms reach up in the air.
Two little feet go jump, jump, jump.
Two little fists go thump, thump, thump.
One little body goes round, round, round,
And one little child sits quietly down.

After a Bath

After my bath, I try, try, try
To wipe myself 'til I'm dry, dry, dry.

Hands to wipe, and fingers and toes,
And two wet legs and a shiny nose.
Just think, how much less time I'd take,
If I were a dog, and could shake, shake, shake.

Helping's Fun

When I come in from outdoor play, (Pretend to open door)
I take my boot off right away. (Remove boots)
I set them by the door just so, (Place them by door)
Then off my cap and mittens go. (Remove cap and mittens)
Zip down my coat and snow pants too, (Remove coat and snow pants)
And hang them up when I am through. (Hang them up)
I'm a helper, don't you see? (Point to self)
Helping's fun, as fun can be. (Clap hands)

Me

My hands upon my head I **place,**
On my shoulders, on my **face.**
On my knees and at my **side,**
Then behind me they will **hide.**
Then I raise them up SO **high,**
'Til they almost reach the **sky.**
Swiftly count them—1, 2, **3,**
And see how quiet they can **be.**

Stand Up Tall

Stand up tall, (Children stand)
Hands in air. (Raise hands)
Now sit down (Children sit)
In your chair.
Clap your hands, (Clap three times)
Make a frown, (Children frown)
Smile and smile, (Children smile)
And flop like a clown. (Children relax whole body with arms dangling)

Elephant

Right foot, left foot, see me go. (Put weight on first one foot, then the
I am gray and big and slow.   other, swaying from side to side)
I come walking down the street
With my trunk and four big feet. (Extend arms together in front and
                                        swing like a trunk)

Helpful Friends

Policeman stands so tall and straight, (Stand up straight)
Holds up his hand for cars to wait. (Hold up right hand)
Blows his whistle, "Tweet, tweet," (Pretend to blow whistle)
'Til I'm safely 'cross the street.
Mailman carries a full pack, (Holds both hands over one shoulder)
Of cards and letters on his back.
Step, step, step, now ring, ring, ring! (Step in place, pretend to ring bell)
What glad surprises will he bring?
Gasman puts gas in our car, (Pretend to pump gas)
So that we can drive it far. (Driving motion)
Washes windows, lifts the hood, (Pretend to wash windows and lift hood)
Checks the oil, his work is good. (Pretend to check oil)
Milkman drives his truck this way, (Pretend to drive truck)
Stops at our house every day. (Point to self)
Brings us cool, fresh milk to drink, (Pretend to drink)
These are helpful friends, I think.

Teddy Bear, Teddy Bear

Teddy Bear, Teddy Bear, (Standing in place, suit actions to words).
Turn around.
Teddy Bear, Teddy Bear,
Touch the ground.
Teddy Bear, Teddy Bear,
Show your shoe.
Teddy Bear, Teddy Bear,
That will do.

Teddy Bear, Teddy Bear,
Go upstairs.
Teddy Bear, Teddy Bear,
Say your prayers.
Teddy Bear, Teddy Bear,
Turn out the light.
Teddy Bear, Teddy Bear,
Say good night!

Index

REFLECTS MORE THAN
10 YEARS OF STUDY IN
KINDERGARTEN AND
FIRST-GRADE CLASSROOMS!

ROAD TO THE CODE
A Phonological Awareness Program for Young Children

By Benita A. Blachman, Ph.D., Eileen Wynne Ball, Ph.D., Rochella Black, M.S., & Darlene M. Tangel, Ph.D.

For kindergartners and first graders who need extra work on their early literacy skills, this proven plan for teaching phonemic awareness and letter–sound correspondences can be a valuable resource in any primary classroom! Expert researchers created this developmentally sequenced, 44-lesson program to give students repeated opportunities to practice and enhance their beginning reading and spelling abilities. Perfect for small groups or individual instruction, **Road to the Code** is easy for teachers to use and understand because it has detailed scripted instructions and photocopiable materials—such as picture cards, letter cards, and games.

$49.95 • 2000 • Stock #4382 • 416 pages • 8¹/₂ x 11 • spiral-bound • ISBN 1-55766-438-2

EXTENSIVELY TESTED—THE *KINDERGARTEN ACTIVITY BOOK* WAS TESTED UNDER RESEARCH AND PRACTICAL CONDITIONS FOR TEN YEARS, AND THE *PRESCHOOL ACTIVITY BOOK* WAS FIELD-TESTED FOR FOUR YEARS IN A VARIETY OF PRESCHOOL SETTINGS.

LADDERS TO LITERACY
A Preschool Activity Book

By Angela Notari-Syverson, Ph.D., Rollanda E. O'Connor, Ph.D., & Patricia F. Vadasy, M.P.H.

The **Preschool Activity Book** targets basic preliteracy skills. It orients children toward printed materials and teaches letter sounds. Developmentally appropriate assessment procedures—informal guidelines, structured performance samples, and a checklist—help educators monitor children's progress.

$49.95 • 1998 • Stock #3173 • 400 pages • 8¹/₂ x 11 • spiral-bound • ISBN 1-55766-317-3

LADDERS TO LITERACY
A Kindergarten Book

By Rollanda E. O'Connor, Ph.D., Angela Notari-Syverson, Ph.D., & Patricia F. Vadasy, M.P.H.

The **Kindergarten Activity Book** focuses on developing preacademic, early literacy, and early reading skills. Goals become more involved as children learn to recognize letters, match sounds with letters, and develop phonological awareness and the alphabetic principle!

$45.95 • 1998 • Stock #3181 • 304 pages • 8¹/₂ x 11 • spiral-bound • ISBN 1-55766-318-1

ORDER BOTH ACTIVITY
BOOKS AND **SAVE!**
LADDERS TO LITERACY (SET)
STOCK #3270 • $86.00

SPEECH TO PRINT
Language Essentials for Teachers
By Louisa Cook Moats, Ed.D.

This thorough and well-written book ties textbook theory to classroom practice, helping readers to discover the connection between language structure and how students learn to read. Working through the exercises will enable educators to recognize, understand, and solve the problems that children encounter when learning to read and write. Complete with case studies; field-tested lesson plans; and extensive appendices including answer keys, **Speech to Print** is the indispensable guide for becoming an effective literacy instructor!

Now available—the **Speech to Print Workbook.** Teachers will expand their knowledge of language with the exercises inside!

Book
$29.95 • 2000 • Stock #3874 • 288 pages • 7 x 10 • paperback • ISBN 1-55766-387-4

Workbook
$19.95 • 2003 • Stock #630X • 176 pages • 8¹/₂ x 11 • paperback • ISBN 1-55766-630-X

BEGINNING LITERACY WITH LANGUAGE
Children Learning at Home and School
Edited by David K. Dickinson, Ed.D., & Patton O. Tabors, Ed.D.

Through research gathered in the Home–School Study of Language and Literacy Development, the authors share the relationship they've found between critical teacher–child and parent–child interactions and children's kindergarten language and literacy skills. In each chapter, educators will read actual transcripts of parents and teachers talking to children during everyday activities, recognize how these interactions relate to later development, and get suggestions for supporting children's language and literacy development throughout the school day.

$29.95 • 2001 • Stock #479X • 432 pages • 6 x 9 • paperback • ISBN 1-55766-479-X

READING IN THE CLASSROOM
Systems for the Observation of Teaching & Learning
Edited by Sharon Vaughn, Ph.D., & Kerri L. Briggs, Ph.D.

Classroom observation is the best way to pinpoint what does and what doesn't work in reading instruction, and this text will help readers choose from nine observations systems available today or design their own system using concepts developed by top researchers. Each chapter explains how the system was developed; includes a detailed description of its field testing, reliability, and validity; examines strengths and limitations; and may include the actual tool discussed. Readers will explore systems that give them the best possible understanding of which approaches to reading instruction are working and what work still needs to be done.

$39.95 • 2003 • Stock #6512 • 320 pages • 6 x 9 • paperback • ISBN 1-55766-651-2

EARLY LANGUAGE & LITERACY CLASSROOM OBSERVATION (ELLCO) TOOLKIT, RESEARCH EDITION

By Miriam W. Smith, Ed.D., & David K. Dickinson, Ed.D., *with Angela Sangeorge & Louisa Anastasopoulos, M.P.P.*

Programs across the country are using **ELLCO,** the first field-tested observation toolkit to specifically address the role of environmental factors in early literacy and language development. Designed for prekindergarten to third grade classrooms, **ELLCO** helps administrators, principals, supervisors, and program directors gather the knowledge schools need to strengthen classroom quality and build better literacy programs.

The **User's Guide** to the *ELLCO Toolkit* contains

- a brief but comprehensive introduction on how to use **ELLCO** in school improvement planning, professional development, and supervision
- step-by-step instructions for each of the toolkit's three parts
- a compelling narrative, *Kenny's Story*, that describes how one teacher sparked a young boy's interest in literacy and explores how teachers can apply these concepts with their own students
- a detailed technical appendix on the research behind **ELLCO** and its psychometric properties

The three-part **ELLCO Toolkit** includes

- The *Literacy Environment Checklist* (15-20 minutes). Users examine the classroom's layout and contents through 25 items that measure availability, content, and diversity of reading, writing, and listening materials.

- The *Classroom Observation and Teacher Interview* (20-45 minutes). Users observe teachers interacting with children and the classroom environment, and rate the quality of classroom supports for literacy through 14 age-specific observation elements. These items cover two general areas: *General Classroom Environment* and *Language, Literacy, and Curriculum*. After the observation is complete, the brief *Teacher Interview* takes less than 10 minutes to help users clarify aspects of the observation.

- The *Literacy Activities Rating Scale* (10 minutes). Users record how many times and for how long nine literacy behaviors occurred in two categories: *Book Reading* and *Writing*.

User's Guide
$30.00 • 2002 • Stock #5729 • 80 pages • 7 x 10 • paperback • ISBN 1-55766-572-9

Toolkit (pack of 5)
$20.00 • 2002 • Stock #5710 • 24 pages each • 8¹/₂ x 11 • saddle-stitched • ISBN 1-55766-571-0

UNLOCKING LITERACY
Effective Decoding and Spelling Instruction
By Marcia K. Henry, Ph.D.

This innovative book gives educators a refresher course on language skills and structure along with a wide range of teaching strategies to help students from prekindergarten to middle school and beyond learn to read and spell accurately. Teachers will sharpen their knowledge of three basic concepts for decoding and spelling words: letter-sound correspondences, syllable patterns, and morpheme patterns. They'll also help students develop print awareness and phonological awareness, understand word parts and origins, and learn about new English words and less common Latin roots and Greek combining forms.

$29.95 • 2003 • Stock #6644 • 320 pages • 7 x 10 • paperback • ISBN 1-55766-664-4